The roses following are picked up
from the old history of paintings,
chinaware, and garments.

Decorative pattern on the plate from Rhodes Island: Instructions on page 57

From "wild rose and a lion" England: Instructions on page 58

Flower motif, early 17th century England: Instructions on page 60

Detail from the gown for the events in Prague: Instructions on page 59

Rose worked on the pendant, portrait of Elizabeth I inside: Instructions on page 62

Above: Detail from a shawl used for baptism: Instructions on page 64

Right above: Decorative pattern from "flower and a butterfly", the Victorian age: Instructions on page 66

Right below: Detail from carpet, Italian: Instructions on page 60

Detail from ''flower and consects'', art crafts Firenze: Instructions on page 62

Decorative pattern from the panel of alter, Wien: Instructions on page 65

Pattern on the pillow, the Elizabethan age: Instructions on page 68   7

Embroidery pattern 17th century in India: Instructions on page 66

Painting on tiles, Turkish: Instructions on page 69

Decorative pattern from India, and Persia: Instructions on page 70

9

Detail on silk skirt from Norway: Instructions on page 70

Decorative pattern, the Victorian 19th century: Instructions on page 72

Drawing from Persia, 18th century: Instructions on page 73

Detail from paper crafts, traditional art in China: Instructions on page 74

ROSES-ROSES
Classic Roses

Tablecloth Instructions on page 75

Runner Instructions on page 77

Tablecloth Instructions on page 79

Tablecloth Instructions on page 81

Tablecloth & Wagon Mat Instructions on page 88

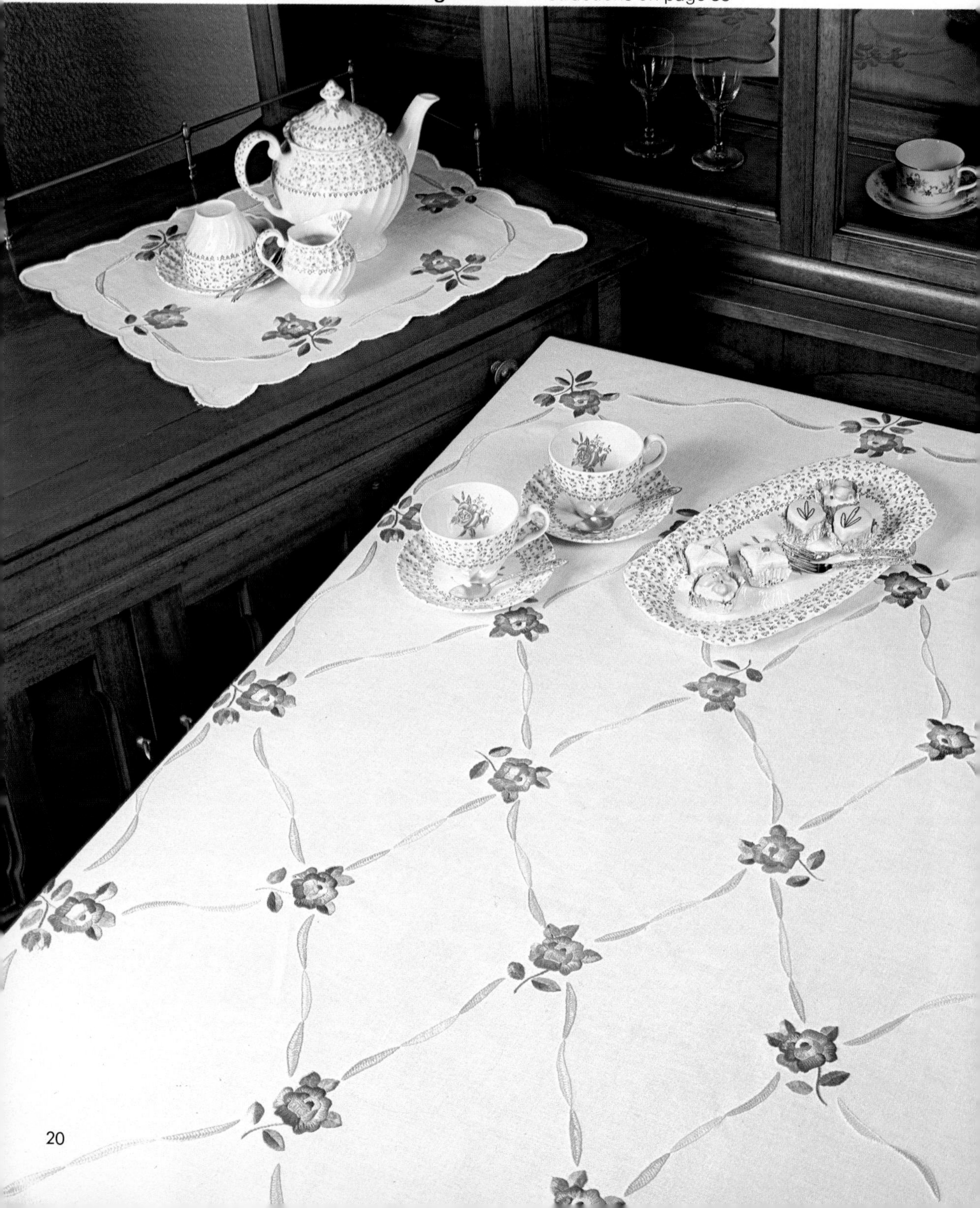

Pillows Instructions on page 91

Doily Instructions on page 96

Lampshade Instructions on page 92

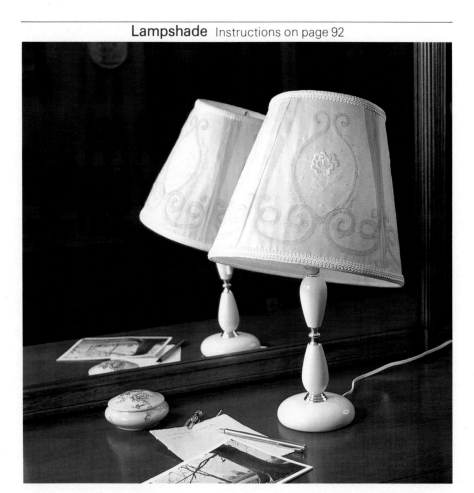

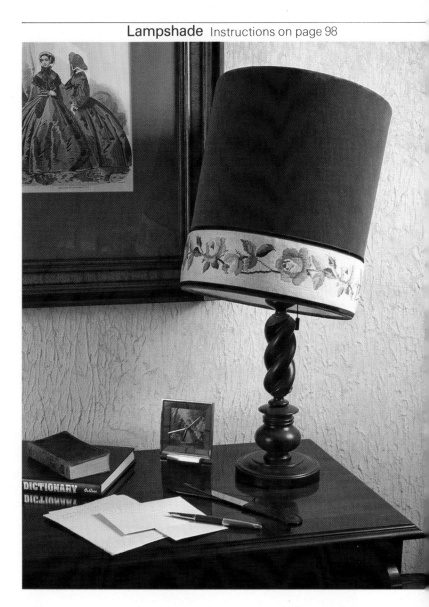

Doily Instructions on page 99

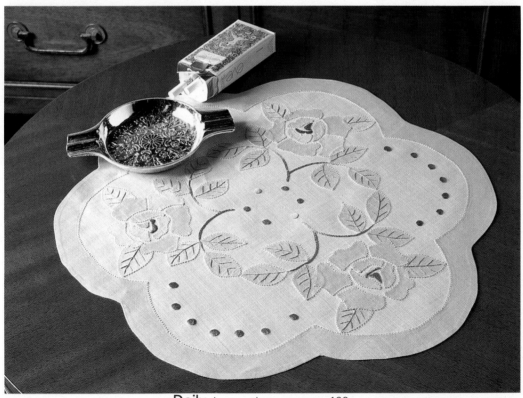

Doily Instructions on page 100

Hand-Mirror & Mini Hanger   Instructions on page 108

Frames Instructions on page 110

Frame Instructions on page 114

Piano Throw Instructions on page 116

Piano Throw Instructions on page 118

Roses–Roses
SURROUNDED BY SWEET ROSES

Piece Spread on Basket & Tray Mat

Instructions on page 126

Center Piece
Instructions on page 123

Doily Instructions on page 128

Luncheon Mats Instructions on page 132

Bedspread

Instructions on page 149

ROSES IN LETTERING

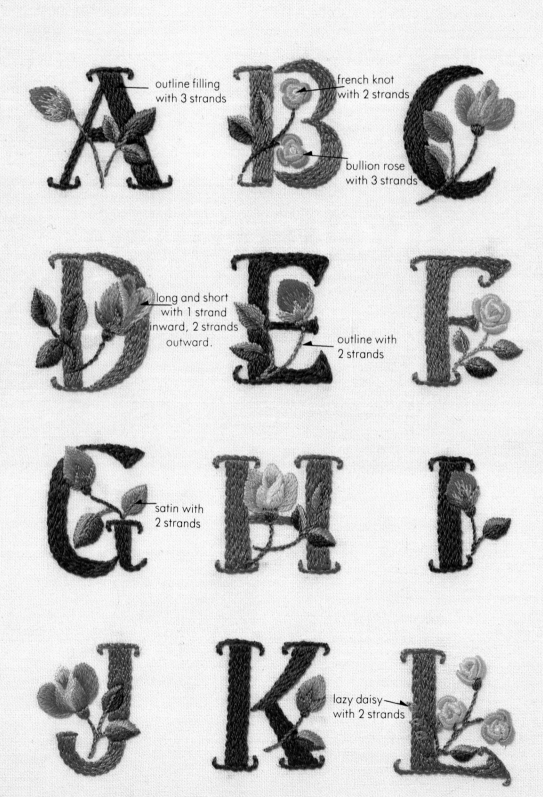

outline filling with 3 strands

french knot with 2 strands

bullion rose with 3 strands

long and short with 1 strand inward, 2 strands outward.

outline with 2 strands

satin with 2 strands

lazy daisy with 2 strands

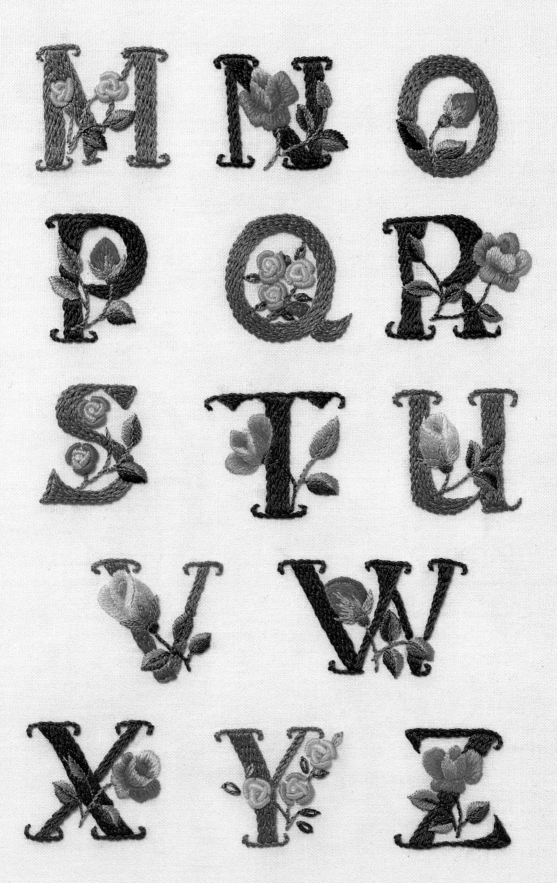

With 3 strands unless specified.

bullion rose

open chain

outline

chain

lazy daisy

satin

long & short
with 2 strands inward

satin

outline filling

long & short

satin

outline

lazy daisy

outline
filling

bullion rose

outline

long & short

outline
filling

french knot

closed
herringbone

outline

satin

With 3 strands unless specified.

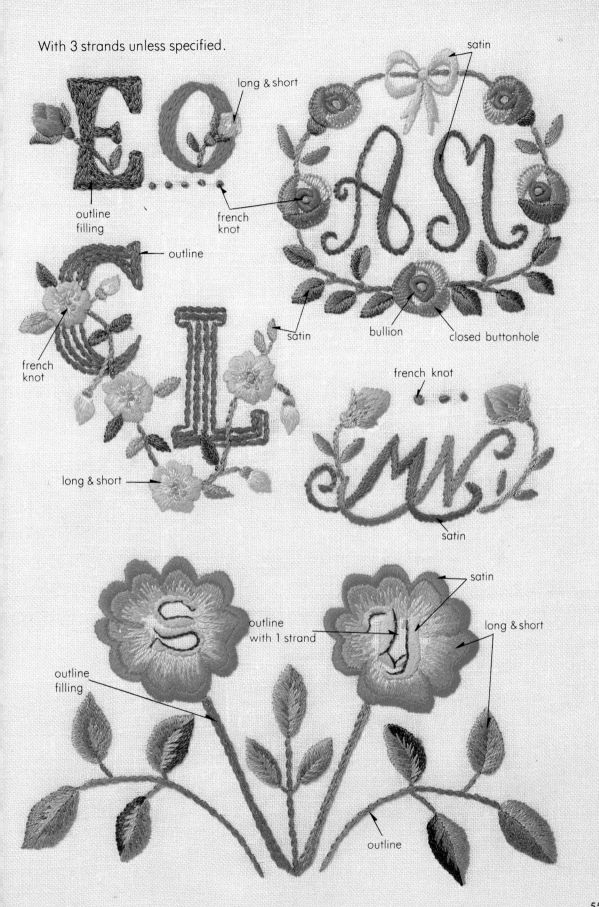

long & short

satin

outline
filling

french
knot

outline

french
knot

satin

bullion

closed buttonhole

long & short

french knot

satin

satin

outline
with 1 strand

long & short

outline
filling

outline

With 3 strands unless specified.

outline

satin

straight

leaf

outline

bullion rose

french knot

lazy daisy

outline

leaf

long & short with 2 strands inward

satin

outline filling

outline

MAKING INSTRUCTIONS

FRAME   shown on page 1

You'll Need
Fabric...White silk.
Threads...D.M.C 6-strand embroidery floss:
1 skein each of Forget-me-not Blue (809, 813, 824, 826), Sky Blue (517, 518, 519), Cornflower Blue (792, 793), Sevres Blue (798, 799), Royal Blue (996), Peacock Green (992, 993), Emerald Green (911, 912, 913, 954), Laurel Green, (987, 989), Pistachio Green (320, 368), Ivy Green (501), Almond Green (502), Jade Green (943), Brilliant Green (704), Cardinal Red (347), Morocco Red (3328), Smoke Grey (644) and Peacock Green (991).

Finished Size: 24 cm wide 26 cm long (size of design)

With 3 strands

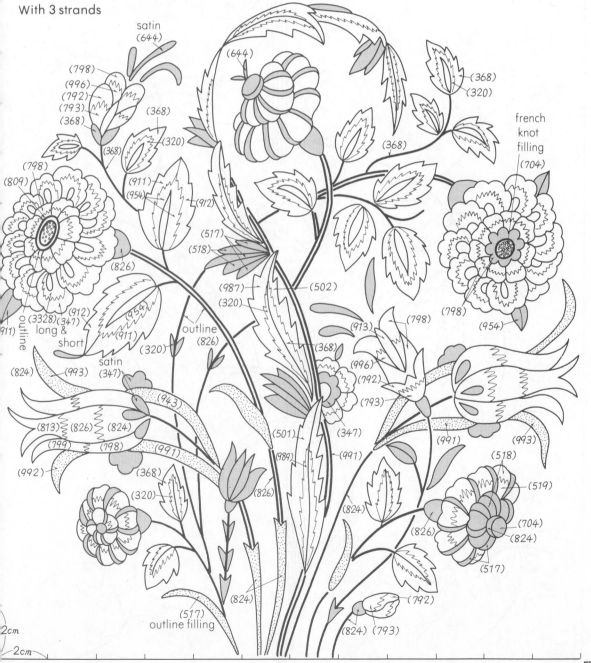

FRAME

shown on page 2 above

You'll Need
Fabric... Grey silk.
Threads...D.M.C 6-strand embroidery floss:
1 skein each of Sage Green (3011, 3012, 3013), Yellow Green (733, 734), Moss Green (471, 472), Almond Green (502), Chocolate (632), Faded Pink (221, 223, 224), Terra-cotta (356, 758), Morocco Red (760, 761, 3328), Cardinal Red (347), Geranium Red (754, 948), Scarlet (498); 1/2 skein each of Beaver Grey (645, 647) and Umber (434).
Finished Sise: 21 cm wide 24 cm long (size of design)

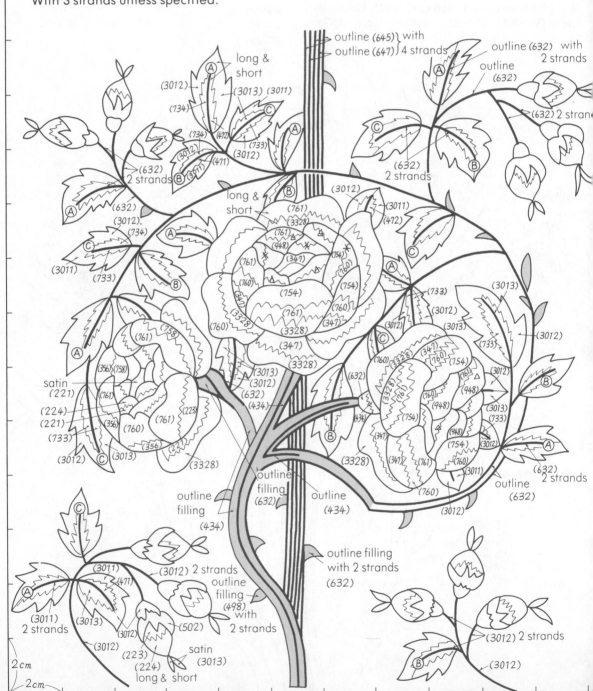

FRAME

shown on page 3 above

You'll Need
Fabric...Ivory linen.
Threads...D.M.C 6-strand embroidery floss: 1 skein each of Dull Mauve (316, 778), Faded

Pink (221, 223, 224, 225), Terra-cotta (356), Sage Green (3011, 3012, 3013) and Green (3051).
Finished Size: 19 cm wide 18 cm long (size of design)

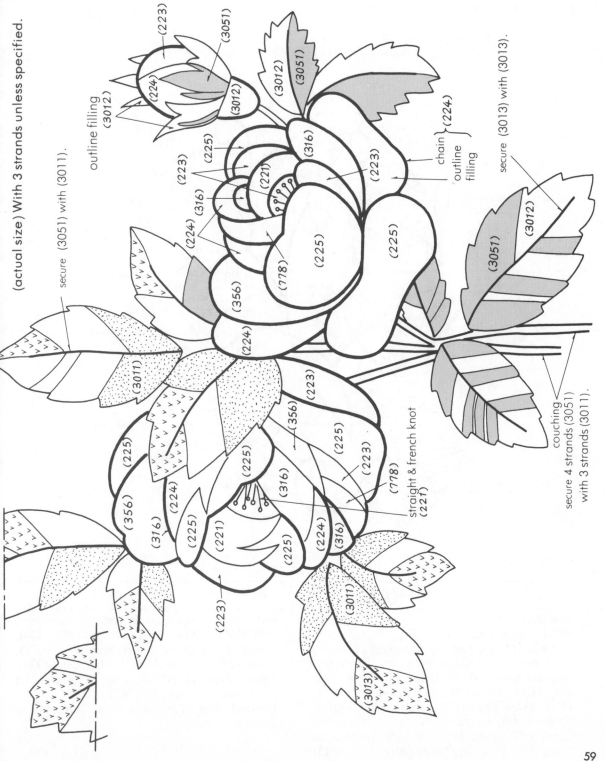

(actual size) With 3 strands unless specified.

outline filling (3012)

secure (3051) with (3011).

chain (224)
outline filling

secure (3013) with (3013).

couching
secure 4 strands (3051)
with 3 strands (3011).

straight & french knot (221)

59

You'll Need
Fabric...Silk Silver Grey.
Threads...D.M.C 6-strand embroidery floss:
1/2 skein each of Sage Green (3012, 3013),
Yellow Green (733, 734), Copper Green (833,
834), Umber (738, 739), Beige (3047), Corn

Yellow (712), Old Gold (676) and Morocco
Red (760, 3328). Small amount of Gold thread.
Finished Size: 8.5 cm wide 11.5 cm long (size of
design)

(actual size)   Long and short stitch,
with 2 strands unless specified.

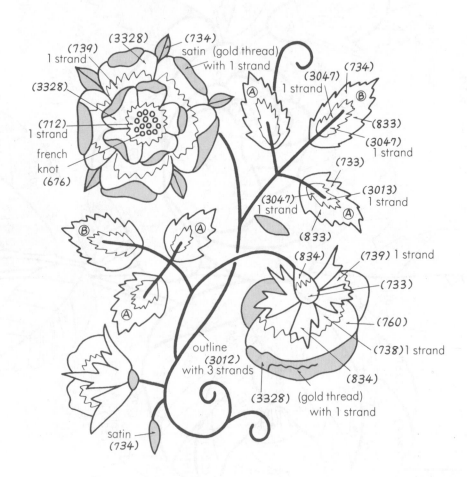

(3328)   (734)
(739)   satin (gold thread)
1 strand   with 1 strand

(3328)

(712)
1 strand

french
knot
(676)

(3047)   (734)
1 strand

(833)

(3047)
1 strand

(733)

(3013)
1 strand

(3047)
1 strand

(833)

(834)   (739) 1 strand

(733)

(760)

(738) 1 strand

(834)

(3328) (gold thread)
with 1 strand

outline
(3012)
with 3 strands

satin
(734)

You'll Need
Fabric...Grey silk.
Threads...D.M.C 6-strand embroidery floss:
1/2 skein each of Garnet Red (309, 326, 335),
Magenta Rose (962, 963), Soft Pink (818, 776,
819, 3326), Scarlet (815), Saffron (725, 726,
727), Golden Yellow (783), Light Yellow (3078),
Cream (746), Green (3051, 3052), Pistachio
Green (320, 368), Ivy Green (501), Almond
Green (502, 503), Sage Green (3011, 3012, 3013)

and White; small amount each of Raspberry
Red (3685, 3687, 3688), Plum (553, 554),
Parma Violet (211), Azure Blue (775, 3325),
Forget-me-not Blue (813), Umber Gold (976),
Yellow Green (732, 733), Copper Green (831)
and Pistachio Green (319, 367).
Finished Size: 21 cm wide 17 cm long (size of
design)

(actual size) With 3 strands

You'll Need
Fabric...Cotton satin Beige.
Threads...D.M.C 6-strand embroidery floss:
1/2 skein each of Turky Red (321), Poppy (666), Scarlet (304), Peacock Green (992) and Beaver Grey (844).
Finished Size: 11 cm wide 10 cm long (size of design)

(actual size) With 2 strands

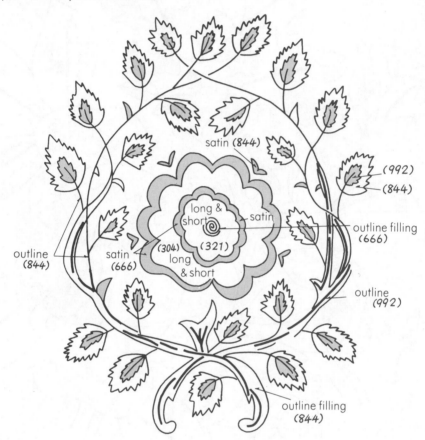

You'll Need
Fabric...Black satin.
Threads...D.M.C 6-strand embroidery floss:
1 skein each of Raspberry Red (3685, 3687, 3688, 3689), Soft Pink (818, 899), Magenta Rose (961, 962, 963), Garnet Rose (309), Old Rose (3350, 3354), Geranium Red (350, 351, 352, 353, 754, 817), Cardinal Red (347), Ivy Green (501), Almond Green (502), Peacock Green (991), Pistachio Green (319, 320, 367, 368, 369) and Laurel Green (987, 988); 1/2 skein each of Azure Blue (775, 3325), Corn Yellow (712), Antique Blue (931, 932), Beige (3046, 3047), Beige Brown (839, 841); small amount each of Forget-me-not Blue (825), Indigo (334), Ash Grey (318, 415), Myrtle Grey (927, 928), Indian Red (3041, 3042), Coffee Brown (938), Old Gold (676, 680, 729), Beige Brown (840), Greenish Grey (597), Mahogany (300, 402), Parrakeet Green (905, 907), Emerald Green (912), Moss Green (471) and Yellow Green (733).
Finished Size: 22.5 cm wide 29 cm long (size of design)

Long & short stitch, with 3 strands unless specified.

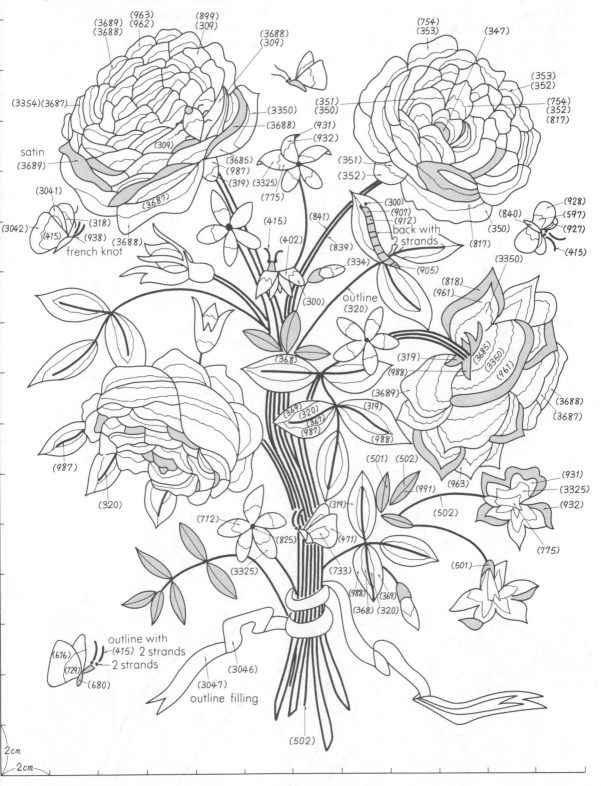

satin
(3689)

french knot

outline
(320)

back with
2 strands

outline with
(415) 2 strands
2 strands

outline filling

2cm
2cm

You'll Need
Fabric... Black satin.
Threads...D.M.C 6-strand embroidery floss:
1 skein each of Raspberry Red (3688, 3689),
Soft Pink (818); 1/2 skein each of Old Rose
(3350, 3354), Magenta Rose (961, 962, 963),
Soft Pink (3326), Pistachio Green (367, 368),

Green (3053), Ivy Green (501), Almond Green
(502), Peacock Green (991, 992), Sage Green
(3012, 3013), Emerald Green (910) and Raspberry Red (3687).
Finished Size: 16.5 cm wide 18.5 cm long (size
of design)

(actual size) With 3 strands unless specified,
with 2 strands inward of long and short stitch.

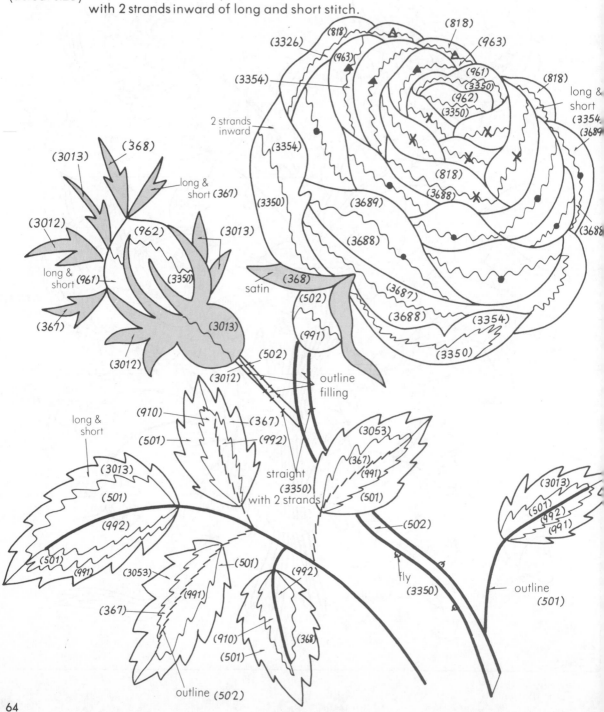

You'll Need
Fabric...Silk Gold Brown.
Threads...D.M.C 6-strand embroidery floss:
1 skein each of Soft Pink (776, 818, 899, 3326), Garnet Red (309, 326, 335), Scarlet (498, 814), Pistachio Green (319), Laurel Green (986, 987, 989), Moss Green (469, 471), Golden Green (580, 581), Scarab Green (3346, 3347, 3348) and Parrakeet Green (905, 907); small amount of Magenta Rose (962).
Finished Size: 16cm wide 17.5cm long (size of design)

Long and short stitch,   (actual size)

with 3 strands unless specified.

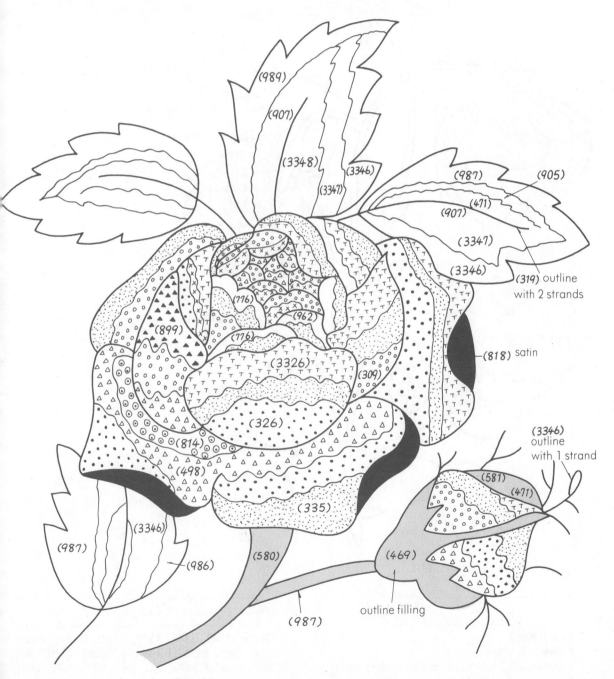

(actual size)

With 3 strands unless specified.

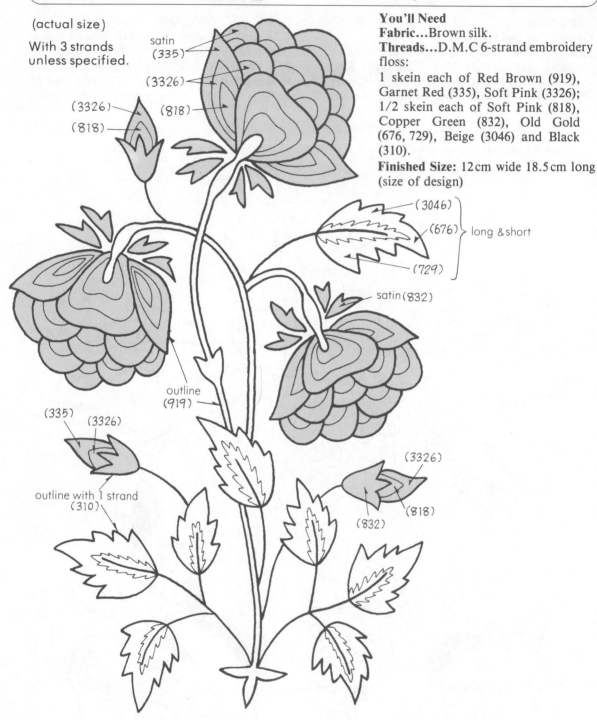

satin (335)

(3326)

(818)

(3326)
(818)

(3046)
(676) } long & short
(729)

satin (832)

outline (919)

(335) (3326)

outline with 1 strand (310)

(3326)

(832) (818)

You'll Need
Fabric... Brown silk.
Threads...D.M.C 6-strand embroidery floss:
1 skein each of Red Brown (919), Garnet Red (335), Soft Pink (3326); 1/2 skein each of Soft Pink (818), Copper Green (832), Old Gold (676, 729), Beige (3046) and Black (310).
Finished Size: 12 cm wide 18.5 cm long (size of design)

You'll Need
Fabric... White silk.
Threads...D.M.C 6-strand embroidery floss:
1 skein each of Moss Green (936), Scarab

Green (3345, 3346, 3347, 3348), Laurel Green (986, 987, 988), Pistachio Green (320, 367, 368), Cerise (600, 601, 602, 603, 604, 605), Soft Pink (818), Raspberry Red (3689), Saffron

(727), Tangerine Yellow (745), Umber (434, 435), Red Brown (918, 919, 920, 921), Terracotta (355, 356), Beige (3045), Coffee Brown (801) and Canary Yellow (971, 972); small amount of Black (310).

Finished Size: 16.5 cm wide 22 cm long (size of design)

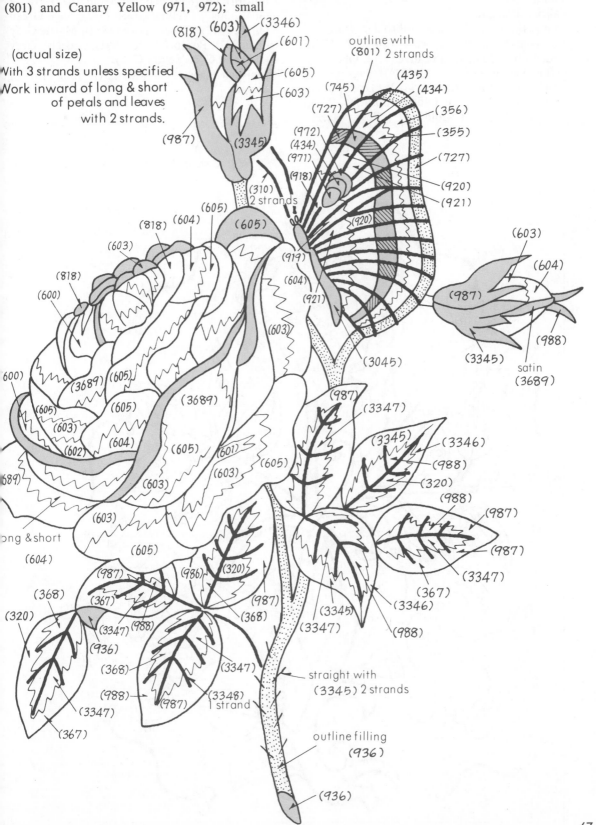

67

FRAME

shown on page 7 below

You'll Need
Fabric...Black satin.
Threads...D.M.C 6-strand embroidery floos:
1/2 skein each of Copper Green (832, 833), Faded Pink (223), Dull Mauve (778), Old Gold (676), Yellow Green (733, 734), Sage Green (3013), Hazel-nut Brown (420), Drab (611); small amount each of Faded Pink (224, 225), Cream (746), Old Gold (677, 729), Hazel-nut Brown (869), Umber Gold (977), Beige (3046, 3047), Yellow Green (732), Sage Green (3011, 3012), Copper Green (834), Myrtle Grey (926, 927), Peacock Green (991), Greenish Grey (598) and Corn Yellow (712).

Finished Size: 19 cm wide 23 cm long (size of design)

With 3 strands unless specified.

68

FRAME

shown on page 9 above

You'll Need
Fabric...Ivory silk.
Threads...D.M.C 6-strand embroidery floss:
1 skein each of Indigo (311, 322, 336), Emerald Green (910, 911), Peacock Green (991); 1/2 skein each of White, Emerald Green (912), Peacock Green (992), Antique Blue (931, 932); small amount each of Peacock Green (993) and Forget-me-not Blue (813).
Finished Size: 20 cm square (size of design)

With **3 strands** unless specified.

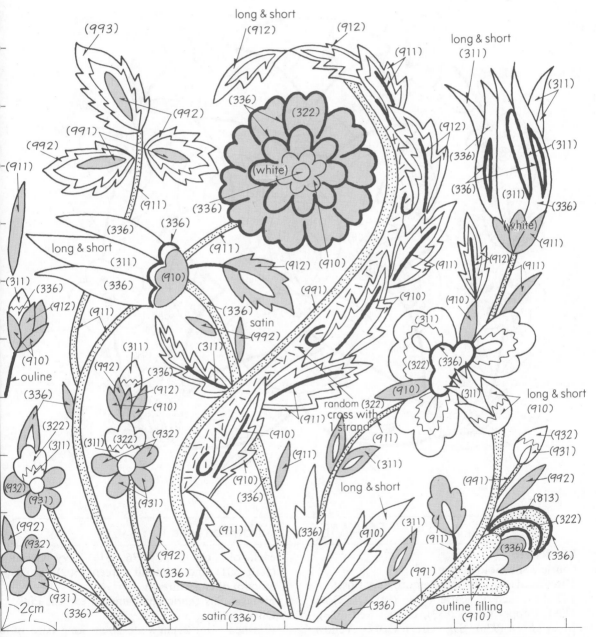

You'll Need
Fabric... Grey silk.
Threads...D.M.C 6-strand embroidery floss:
1/2 skein each of Flame Red (606, 608), Fire Red (946), Canary Yellow (971, 972), Forget-me-not Blue (824, 825), Beige Brown (839),

Old Gold (676), Drab (612, 613), Ash Grey (318), Geranium Red (817), Indian Red (3041, 3042) and Corn Yellow (712).
Finished Size: 13 cm wide 12.5 cm long (size of design)

(actual size)

With **3** strands unless specified
Work inward of long & short with 2 strands.

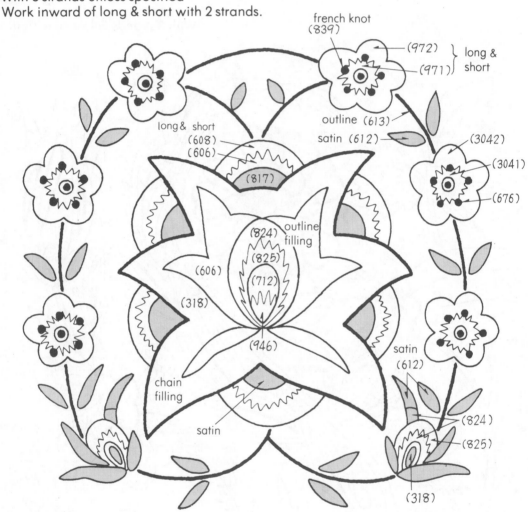

You'll Need
Fabric... Silk Gold Brown.
Threads...D.M.C 6-strand embroidery floss:
1/2 skein each of Scarlet (498, 814), Old Gold (729), Copper Green (833), Garnet Red (326), Moss Green (936), Sage Green (3012), Yellow Green (733), Faded Pink (223, 224, 225), Dull Mauve (778), Green (3051, 3052); small amount

each of Soft Pink (776, 819), Ivy Green (500, 501) and Almond Green (502). Small amount of Gold thread.
Fittings... Silk fabric small amount each of Pink, Olive Green.
Finished Size: 21 cm wide 20 cm long (size of design)

(actual size)
Satin stitch, with 3 strands unless specified

outline with
(305½2 strands)

(326)

(225)

french knot
with 1 strand
(gold thread)

(814)

long & short (3051) (3052)

(819)
(776)
long &
short

(gold thread)

(3012)

(729)

(729)

(936)

(498)

(225)
(814)

(223)

(224)

(778)

(729)

(225)

(498)

(778)

(3052)

(3051)

(814)   (225)   (498)

(326)

(gold thread)
1 strand

(224)

(223)

(936)

(3012)

(501)

(500)

double cross
(502) with 2 strands

(733)

(833)

(936)

(gold thread)
1 strand

(498)

(225)

= silk fabric pink

= silk fabric olive green

71

FRAME

shown on page 11 above

You'll Need
Fabric... Ivory linen.
Threads...D.M.C 6-strand embroidery floss:
1 skein each of Smoke Grey (642), Drab (613), Umber Gold (976), Saffron (725, 726), Golden Yellow (783), Canary Yellow (971), Fire Red (946), Beige Brown (839), Parrakeet Green

(905), Brilliant Green (702, 703, 704), Geranium Red (349, 350, 351, 352, 353, 817), Laurel Green (986), Scarab Green (3345), Plum (552, 553), Episcopal Purple (718, 917) and Scarlet (498); small amount of Black (310).
Finished Size: 16cm square (size of design)

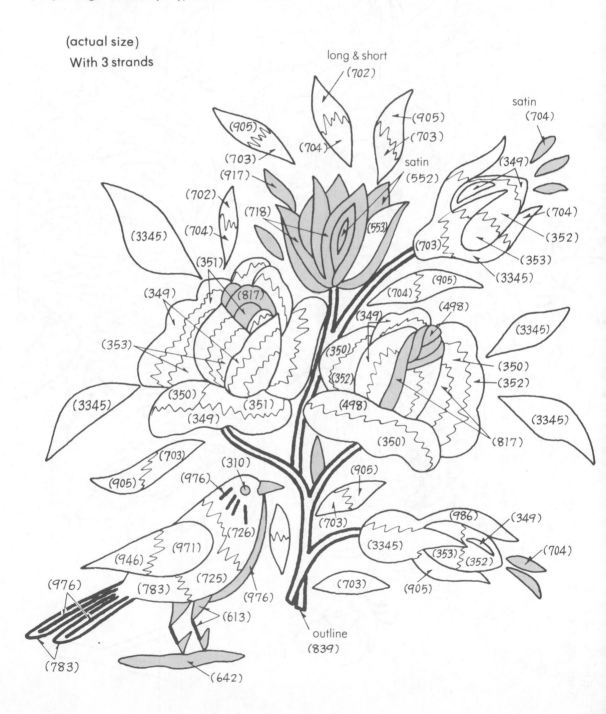

(actual size)

With 3 strands

FRAME
shown on page 11 below

You'll Need
Fabric... Silk Gold Brown.
Threads...D.M.C 6-strand embroidery floss:
1/2 skein each of White, Soft Pink (818, 819), Morocco Red (760, 761, 3328), Cardinal Red (347), Scarab Green (3346, 3348), Golden Green (581), Moss Green (471, 472), Yellow Green (734), Sage Green (3012, 3013), Pistachio Green (319, 320, 367, 368), Green (3051),

Myrtle Grey (924, 926, 927), Drab (611), Silver Grey (3072, 3078), Sky Blue (747), Umber Gold (975), Beaver Grey (844), Ash Grey (318) and Beige (3021).
Finished Size: 10cm wide 13cm long (size of design)

(actual size)
Long & short,
with 2 strands unless specified.

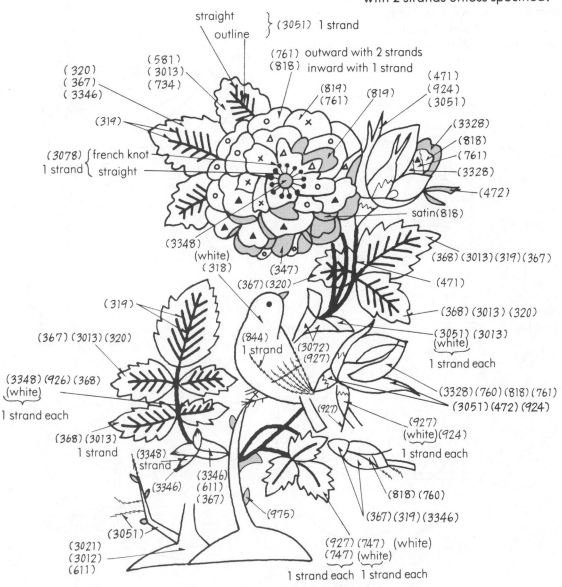

You'll Need

Fabric…Silk Gold Brown.

Threads…D.M.C 6-strand embroidery floss: 1 skein each of Geranium Red (353, 754, 948), Old Gold (676, 677), Drab (613), Smoke Grey (822), Beige (3046, 3047), Yellow Green (734), Laurel Green (987, 988, 989), Moss Green (471), Green (3051, 3052, 3053), Pistachio Green (320, 368), Ivy Green (500, 501), Almond Green (502, 503), Beige Brown (839, 840), Beaver Grey (844), Saffron (725, 726), Drab (611), Golden Yellow (783), Sky Blue (517), Sevres Blue (798, 800), Peacock Blue (799, 806), Forget-me-not Blue (826, 828), Cornflower Blue (793), Brilliant Green (702) and White; small amount each of Scarlet (814), Emerald Green (909), Brilliant Green (701, 703), Cornflower Blue (792), Coffee Brown (898), Soft Pink (819) and Black (310).

Finished Size: 26 cm wide 27 cm long (size of design)

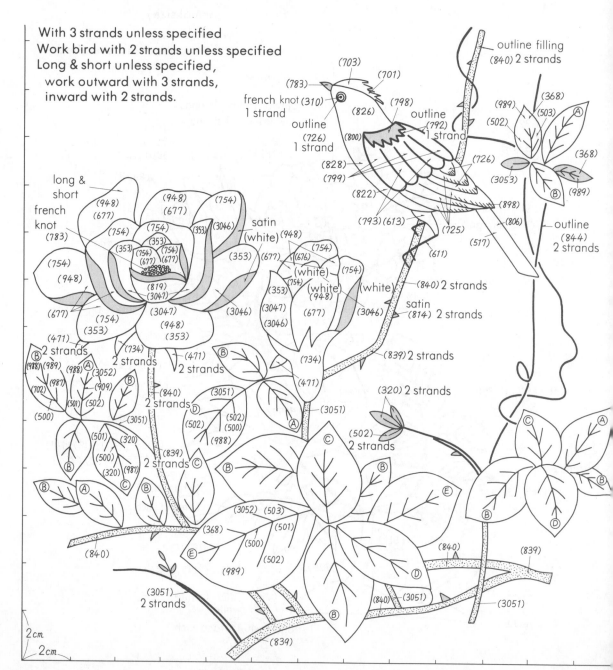

With 3 strands unless specified
Work bird with 2 strands unless specified
Long & short unless specified,
  work outward with 3 strands,
  inward with 2 strands.

You'll Need
Fabrics... Linen: Old Gold 180cm by 130cm, White light weight 90cm square.
Threads...D.M.C 6-strand embroidery floss: 7 skeins of White.
Finished Size: 170cm by 121cm

Making Instructions:
Cut Old Gold linen putting 4.5cm allowance to the measurements indicated on the chart. Fold the allowance into 3.5cm wide on right side mitering corners, secure with punchwork.
Cut each pattern out putting 0.3cm allowance all around, press in shape, turning allowances to wrong side. Punchwork in position with 1 strand.

Chart on Measurements

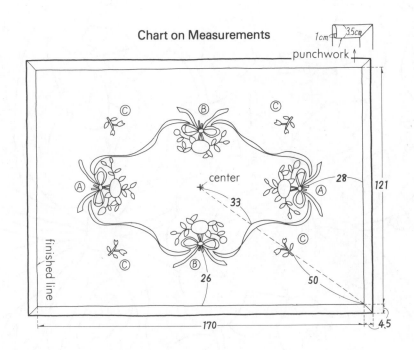

Punchwork

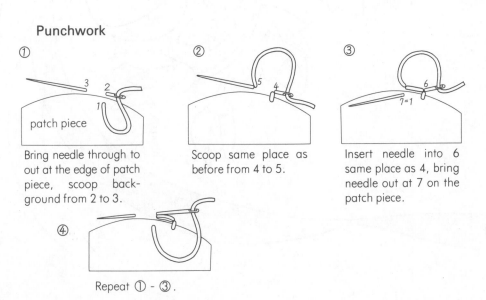

① Bring needle through to out at the edge of patch piece, scoop background from 2 to 3.

② Scoop same place as before from 4 to 5.

③ Insert needle into 6 same place as 4, bring needle out at 7 on the patch piece.

④ Repeat ① - ③.

© A only

satin with 2 strands

B only

punchwork with 1 strand

panchwork

ribbon of A

ribbon of B

3cm

3cm

3cm

You'll Need:

Fabrics…Light weight linen: White 110cm by 70cm, Apple Green, Pale Blue 26cm square each, Blue 21cm square.

Threads…D.M.C 6-strand embroidery floss: 1 skein of White; 1/2 skein each of Pistachio Green (368), Almond Green (504), Forget-me-not Blue (813); small amount each of Indigo (334) and Azure Blue (775, 3325).

Finished Size: 33cm by 104cm in oval

Making Instructions

Cut 2 pieces from White putting 0.5cm allowance to the measurements on the chart, sew into size. Scallop border piece putting 0.3cm allowance, punchwork in position.

Enlarge design, cut pieces out from each color with 0.3cm allowance, punchwork in position.

Chart on Measurements

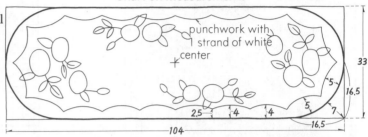

Punchwork with 1 strand,
work the rest with 2 strands

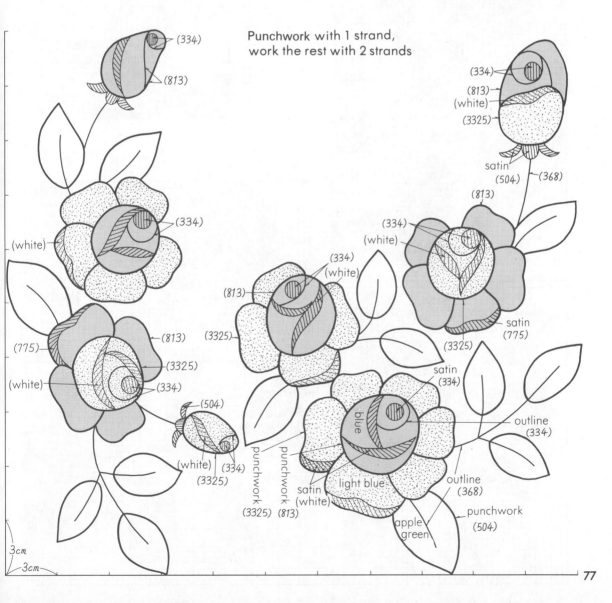

TABLECLOTH

shown on page 16

You'll Need

Fabric... Heavy weight White linen (9 threads per 1 cm) 152 cm by 120 cm.

Threads...D.M.C 6-strand embroidery floss:
6 skeins each of Soft Pink (3326), Laurel Green (988, 989); 4 skeins each of Brilliant Green (704), Ivy Green (501), Garnet Red (309), Raspberry Red (3688); 3 skeins of Laurel Green (986); 2 skeins each of Garnet Red (335), Green (3051), Soft Pink (818), Raspberry Red (3687, 3689); 1 skein each of Raspberry Red (3685), Soft Pink (819) and Scarlet (498).

Fittings...1.5 cm wide White braid 530 cm long.

Finished Size: 146 cm by 114 cm

Making Instructions

Work cross stitch where indicated with 4 strands, counting 2-thread square as a square design on the chart.

Fold the allowance all around twice to wrong side mitering at corners, apply braid on right side, machine steady.

=3326 O = 988
=335 X = 704
=818 △ = 501
=309 — =3689
=498 S =3688
=3051 Ø =3687
=989 ▲ =3685   (square of design =
=986 V = 819   2-thread square of fabric)

center

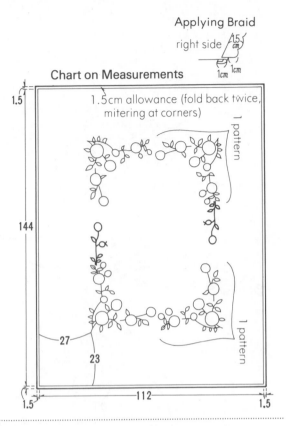

Applying Braid

right side

Chart on Measurements

1.5

1.5 cm allowance (fold back twice, mitering at corners)

1 pattern

144

1 pattern

27

23

1.5

112

1.5

TABLECLOTH   shown on page 15

You'll Need

Fabrics... White linen light weight 90 cm square.

Threads...D.M.C Abroder No. 20 White 9 skeins.

Fittings...2.5 cm wide White braid 370 cm long.

Finished Size: 90 cm square

Making Instructions

Enlarge design, apply on 4 places, work all with 1 strand. Turn cut edge 0.5 cm all around to right side, apply lace overlapping for about 1 cm, edge machine steady. Sew the fold beneath to the wrong side of lace.

Chart on Measurements

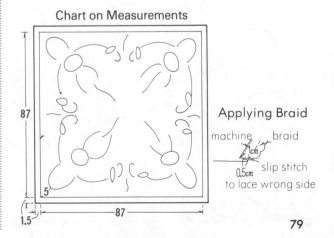

87

5

1.5

87

Applying Braid

machine   braid

slip stitch
0.5cm   to lace wrong side

Overcast Running Stitch

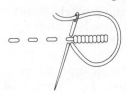

Scoop running stitch closely at right angles to it.

Sewing Bar Across

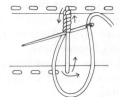

Running stitch the other side. On the way of running stitch this side, make a bar across the ditch where indicated, working buttonhole stitch over the thread stitched acrross.

long & short

overcast running

shadow

satin

outline

satin

closed buttonhole
make a bar across
(buttonhole st)

cut out

with 1 strand

80

You'll Need
Fabrics... White linen 88 cm square.
Threads...D.M.C 6-strand embroidery floss:
3 skeins each of Smoke Grey (644), Soft Pink
(818); 2 skeins each of Old Gold (677), Geranium
Pink (893); 1 skein each of Geranium Pink
(891, 892, 894), Garnet Red (309), Indigo (335),
Soft Pink (776, 899, 3326), Turkey Red (321),
Scarlet (304), Raspberry Red (3685, 3687,
3688, 3689), Peony Rose (956), Beige (3045,
3046), Smoke Grey (822), Azure Blue (775),
Forget-me-not Blue (828), Antique Blue (932),
Tangerine Yellow (743), Plum (554), Parma
Violet (210, 211), Indian Red (3042),
Pistachio Green (320, 367, 368,
369), Moss Green (471),
Sage Green (3011, 3012, 3013),
Yellow Green (733, 734) and White.

Finished Size: 80 cm square
Making Instructions
Enlarge design, work in position. Fold cut edge
all around twice into 2.5 cm wide on wrong side
mitering at every corner, finished with oneside-
hemstitching.

Chart on Measurements

**Color scheme
of leaf**

outward   inward
① (3012) (3013)
② (733)   (471)
③ (471)   (734)
④ (3011) (734)

with 3 strands,
inward of long & short
with 2 strands

You'll Need

Fabric... Aida cloth (52-thread square per 10 cm) White 106 cm by 30 cm.

Threads...D.M.C 6-strand embroidery floss: 3 skeins each of Ash Grey (318, 415); 2 skeins each of Parakeet Green (905), Brilliant Green (704); 1 skein each of Scarab Green (3345), Soft Pink (776, 818, 3326), Magenta Rose (962),

Raspberry Red (3687, 3688, 3689), Old Rose (3350), Episcopal Purple (915), Geranium Pink (894), Peony Rose (956) and Cerise (600, 602, 605).

Fittings...1.5 cm wide braid 270 cm long.

Finished Size: 105 cm by 29 cm

Making Instructions

Referring to chart, work cross stitch and running

running stitch (318)

holbein (962)

holbein (600)

holbein (3687)

holbein (915)

holbein (3350)

⊡	= 818
Ⅱ	= 776
⊠	= 962
⋀	= 3326
◿	= 3689
◪	= 3688
■	= 3350
⊞	= 3687
●	= 915
○	= 894
Ⅲ	= 956
⊂	= 605
▽	= 602
▼	= 600
◉	= 415
⊕	= 318
⊖	= 704
⊗	= 905
⊥	= 3345

↑ 115 sts

center

stitch with 4 strands, holbein stitch with 2 strands.
Finish design in symmetry except the roses on
top and bottom.
Finish all around applying braid on.

Chart on Measurements

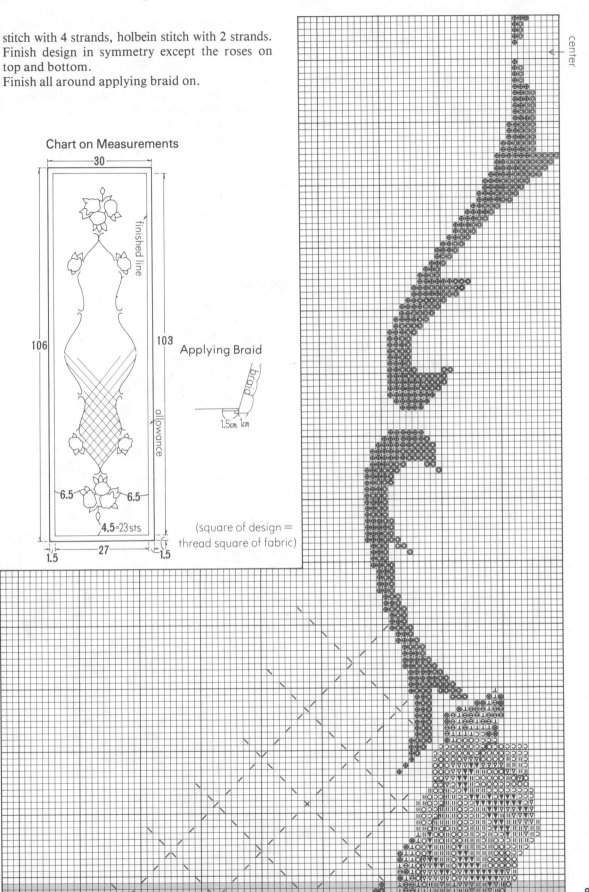

106   103

finished line

allowance

30

6.5   6.5

4.5 = 23 sts

1.5   27   1.5

center

Applying Braid

braid

1.5cm 1cm

(square of design =
thread square of fabric)

You'll Need (for each)

Fabric...Pattern-wove Ivory silk 90 cm by 78 cm.

Threads...D.M.C 6-strand embroidery floss:
2 skeins each of Beige (3045), Umber (738); 1-1/2 skeins of Hazel-nut Brown (869); 1 skein each of Ivy Green (500, 501), Almond Green (502, 503), Green (3051, 3052, 3053), Moss Green (935, 936), Geranium Red (349, 350, 351, 352, 353, 817), Scarlet (304, 498, 814, 815, 816, 902), Garnet Red (309, 335), Soft Pink (776, 899, 3326); small amount each

of Tangerine Yellow (742) and Garnet Red (326).

Fittings...37 cm long zip. 520 g of cased in kapok. Small amount of worsted weight yarn.

Finished Size: Refer to chart.

Making Instructions

Cut fabric out, apply design on front, work embroidery. Sew frill referring to chart, stitch to position.

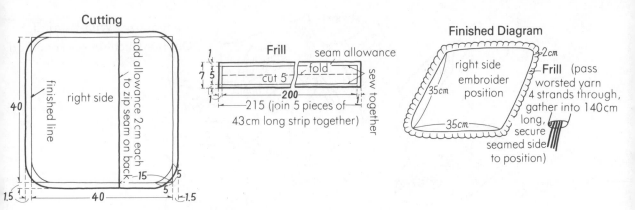

Cutting

finished line

right side

add allowance 2cm each to zip seam on back.

40

1.5   40   5   5   1.5

15

Frill

seam allowance

fold

cut 5

7   5

1   1

200

215 (join 5 pieces of 43cm long strip together)

sew together

Finished Diagram

right side embroider position

35cm

35cm

2cm

Frill (pass worsted yarn 4 strands through, gather into 140cm long, secure seamed side to position)

FRAME   shown on page 23

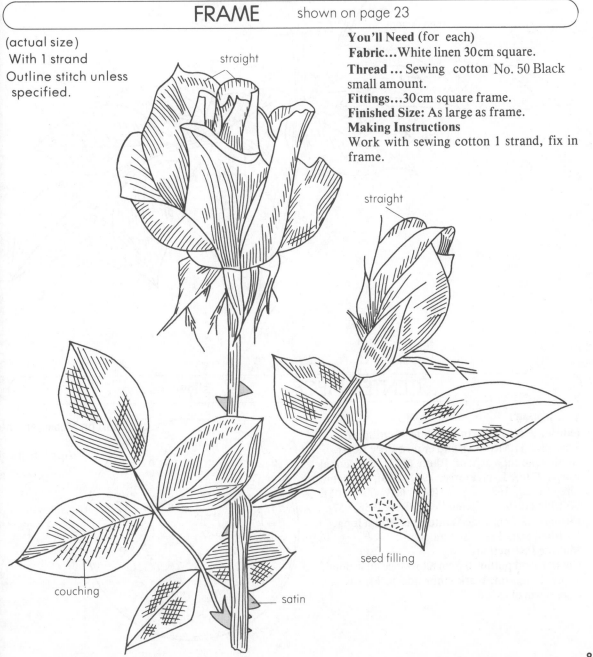

(actual size)
With 1 strand
Outline stitch unless specified.

straight

straight

seed filling

couching

satin

You'll Need (for each)
Fabric... White linen 30cm square.
Thread ... Sewing cotton No. 50 Black small amount.
Fittings...30cm square frame.
Finished Size: As large as frame.
Making Instructions
Work with sewing cotton 1 strand, fix in frame.

satin

straight

(actual size) With 1 strand
Outline stitch unless specified.

seed filling

CENTER PIECE

shown on page 21

You'll Need
Fabric…Cotton organdy White 53 cm square.
Threads…D.M.C 6-strand embroidery floss:
small amount each of Plum (553), Episcopal
Purple (718), Laurel Green (987, 988), Pistachio
Green (320, 368), Cerise (601, 603, 604, 605),
Soft Pink (818, 3326) and Peony Rose (956, 957).
Fittings…2.5 cm wide White lace 180 cm long.
Finished Size: 55 cm in diameter
Making Instructions
Cut in round putting 0.5 cm allowance all around,
apply design on, work embroidery. Finish raw
edge sewing lace on.

Chart on Measurements

Applying Lace

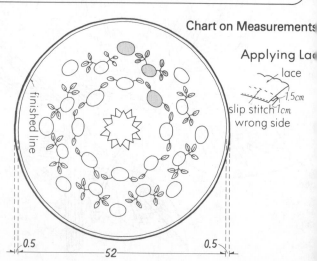

lace

1.5 cm
slip stitch 1cm
wrong side

finished line

0.5   52   0.5

86

(actual size) With 1 strand

Shadow stitch
unless specified

(605)
(818)
(604)
(604)
(603) (603) (604)
(604)

(368)
(320)
(320)
(320)
back (368)

(3326)
(818)
(957)
(956) (956)
(957)
(957)

(320)
(320)
(368)
(368)
(320)
(957)

(987)
(987)

(603)
(604)
(601)
(605)
(603)
(601)
(603)

(988)
(988)

(718)

(553)

center

You'll Need

Fabric...White linen 164cm by 118cm for tablecloth, 53cm by 41cm for wagon mat.

Threads...D.M.C 6-strand embroidery floss: 4-1/2 skeins of Old Gold (676); 4 skeins of Old Gold (677); 2-1/2 skeins each of Pistachio Green (320), White; 2 skeins each of Raspberry Red (3685, 3687, 3688, 3689), Scarab Green (3347, 3348); 1-1/2 skeins each of Pistachio Green (367, 368), Garnet Red (326); 1 skein each of Cerise (601, 602, 603, 604, 605), Garnet Red (309), Magenta Rose (962), Old Rose (3354); 1/2 skein each of Scarab Green (3345, 3346), Soft Pink (776, 818, 3326), Peony Rose (956, 957), Peacock Green (992, 993), Episcopal Purple (718) and Dull Mauve (315). Sewing cotton No. 60 White.

Finished Size: Tablecloth: 154cm by 108cm Wagon Mat: 49cm by 37cm

Making Instrucitons

Copy design referring to "chart on measurements", work embroidery. Finish out edges of tablecloth working oneside-hemstitching with sewing cotton 1 strand, work buttonhole stitch along the out line of wagon mat with 3 strands White, cut off the surplus.

Chart on Measurements (wagon mat)

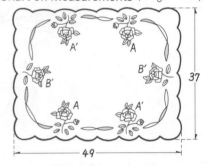

Chart on Measurements (tablecloth)

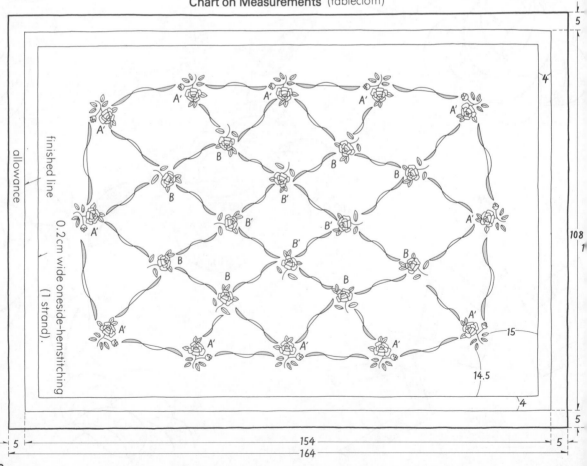

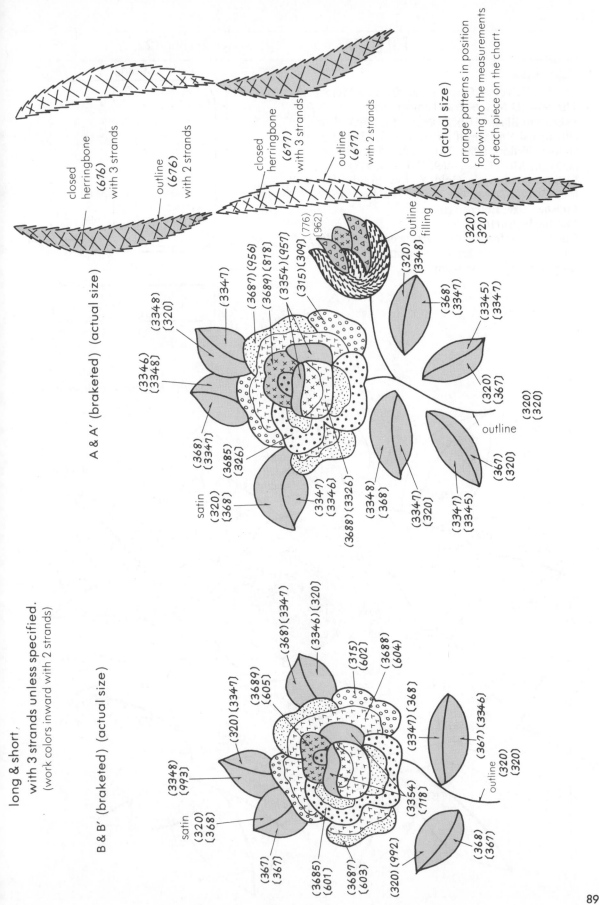

long & short.
with 3 strands unless specified.
(work colors inward with 2 strands)

B & B' (braketed) (actual size)

A & A' (braketed) (actual size)

closed herringbone (676) with 3 strands

outline (676) with 2 strands

closed herringbone (677) with 3 strands

outline (677) with 2 strands

(actual size)
arrange patterns in position following to the measurements of each piece on the chart.

PILLOW

shown on page 22

You'll Need

Fabric…Velveteen Olive Green 90 cm by 73 cm.

Threads…D.M.C 6-strand embroidery floss:
3 skeins of Black (310); 2 skeins of Light Yellow (3078); 1 skein each of Saffron (725, 726, 727), Golden Yellow (780, 781, 782, 783), Umber (433) and Moss Green (469, 470, 935, 937).

Fittings…3 cm wide Gold Yellow braid 170 cm long. 500 g of cased in kapok. 37 cm long zip.

Finished Size: Refer to chart.

Making Instrucitons

Cut fabric referring to chart, work embroidery on front. Secure braid in position, sew into shape putting frill between.

Cutting

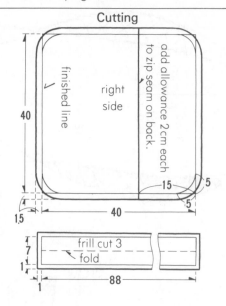

finished line

right side

add allowance 2 cm each to zip seam on back.

40

40

15

5

5

1.5

frill cut 3
fold

7

1

88

1

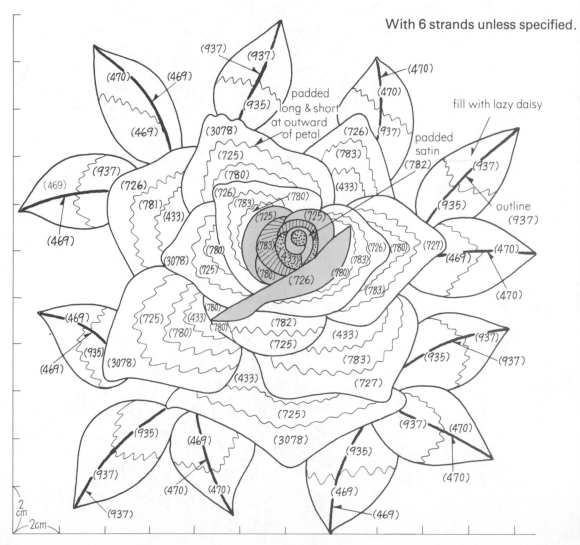

With 6 strands unless specified.

(937) (937)
(470) (469)
(935)
(469)
padded long & short at outward of petal
(3078)
(725)
(780)
(726)
(726) (780)
(783)
(937)
(726)
(781) (433)
(725) (725)
(783) (433)
(433) (780)
(3078) (780)
(725) (725)
(780)
(726)
(469)
(935)
(3078)
(725) (433)
(780) (780)
(782)
(725)
(433)
(783)
(935)
(469)
(935) (3078)
(433)

(470)
(470)
(726) (937)
(783)
(433)
padded satin (782)
fill with lazy daisy
(937)
(935)
outline (937)
(727) (469) (470)
(726) (780) (727)
(783)
(783)
(470)
(782)
(433)
(727)
(937) (937)
(935)
(725)
(937) (470)
(3078)
(935)
(937)
(470)
(469)
(470) (470)
(469)
(937)
(469)

2 cm
2cm

90

Couching

place 3 ply of 6-strand Black
in position, secure with 2 strands.

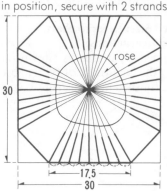

rose

30

30

17.5

Finished Diagram

join 3 pieces of frill into length,
fold in half lengthway, insert between.

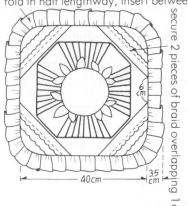

6 cm

40cm

35 cm

secure 2 pieces of braid overlapping 1 cm.

PILLOWS

shown on page 24

You'll Need (for each)
Fabric...Pink (Blue) linen 125 cm by 60 cm.
Thread ... D.M.C 6-strand embroidery floss:
13 skeins of White.
Fittings...40 cm long zip. Fabric for inner case
same size as out piece. 450 g of kapok.
Finished Size: 50 cm square

Chart on Measurements

0.5 cm wide chevron stitch
4 strands.

finished line

50

4

machine back
piece together!

2

2

50

12

zip position on back.

With 3 strands unless specified

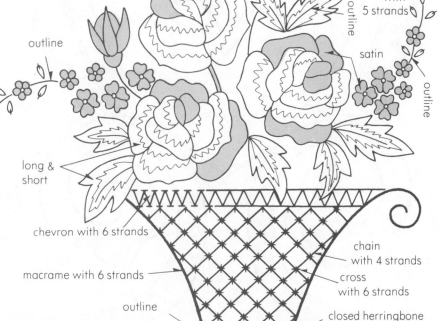

satin

lazy daisy
with
5 strands

outline

satin

outline

outline

outline

long &
short

chevron with 6 strands

macrame with 6 strands

chain
with 4 strands

cross
with 6 strands

outline

closed herringbone

2 cm

2 cm

Making Instructions

Enlarge design,
arrange in position
referring to chart,
work embroidery.
Work chevron sti-
tch around, sew
into shape. Ma-
chine along the out
side of chevron
stitch together
with back piece,
stuff cased in
kapok into.

LAMPSHADE

shown on page 27

You'll Need
Fabric... Cotton organdy Light Purple 90cm by 30cm.
Threads...D.M.C 6-strand embroidery floss:
1 skein of Parma Violet (210); 1/2 skein of White.
Fittings...1cm wide White braid 150cm long.

Finished Size: Refer to chart.
Making Instructions:
Embroider 4 patterns as shown on the chart, altering the facing side of center rose.
Have it finished in lampshade at specialty store.

(actual size)
Shadow stitch, (210)
unless specified.
With 1 strand

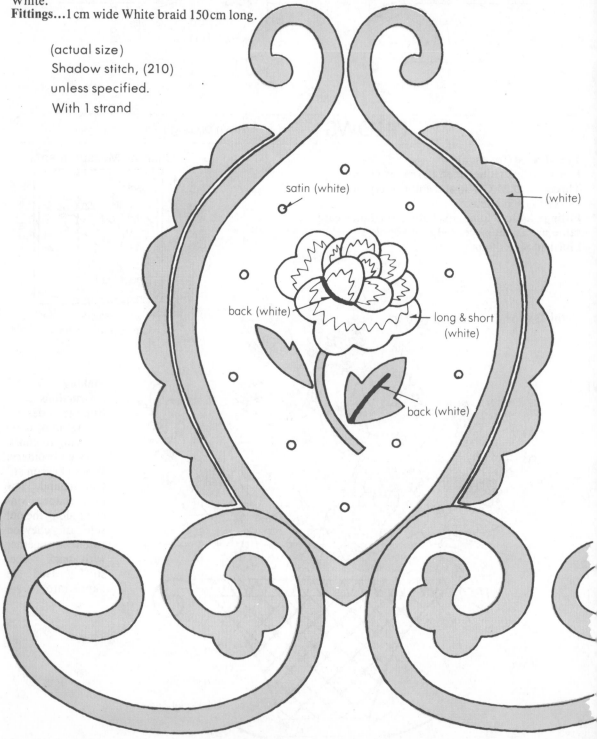

satin (white)

(white)

back (white)

long & short (white)

back (white)

Chart on Measurements

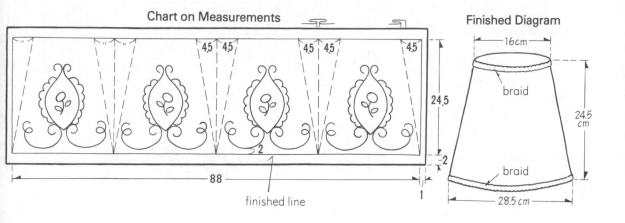

4.5 4.5   4.5 4.5   4.5

24.5

2

88

finished line

Finished Diagram

16cm

braid

braid

24.5 cm

28.5 cm

2

1

PILLOWS

shown on page 28

You'll Need
(for each, bracketed for Brown pillow)
Fabrics...Single canvas (5 threads per 1 cm) 40 cm square. Velveteen Moss Green (Brown) 90 cm by 110 cm.
Threads...D.M.C Tapisserie wool:
10 skeins of Light Grey (7928) [Beige Brown (7460)]; 2 skeins each of Almond Green (7541)[Drab (7487)], Ivy Green (7542) [Old Gold (7485)], Ivy Green (7540)[Hazel-nut Brown (7477)].
For Both 1 skein each of Coffee Brown (7467), Scarab Green (7769), Pink (7375, 7212, 7210), Raspberry Red (7205, 7204), Soft Pink (7132), Scarlet (7115), Raspberry Red (7207, 7758, 7759, 7761, 7191), Yellow (7781, 7782, 7784), Saffron (7726, 7727), Light Yellow (7745,

7890), Pistachio Green (7386), Golden Green (7364, 7583), Scarab Green (7771).
Fittings...42 cm long zip. 1.5 cm wide Dark Gold braid 110 cm long. 500 g of kapok stuffed in 50 cm square case. 2 m long string made of 10 threads of heavy weight yarn.
Finished Size: 53 cm square
Making Instructions
Fix center on canvas, work half-cross stitch picking up each thread with 1 strand. Having worked whole design, fill the space inward of 34 cm circle with straight stitch.
Cut the decorated canvas into 34 cm circle, apply on front, secure with braid so that the inside of diameter becomes 32 cm. Sew into shape referring to chart.

Cutting

frill   1 1 10

"

"

"

2

1.5   49   front   back

49   34

2.5

back 15
      2.5

110

90

Finished Diagram

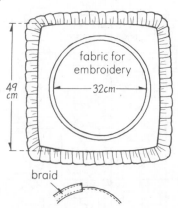

fabric for embroidery

32cm

49 cm

braid

machine decorated piece in position,
put braid over, machine steady.

Frill join 4 pieces together, sew into pipe,
pass yarn-string through,
gather up to the length of
the out edge of pillow.

gather
seam side

93

Center

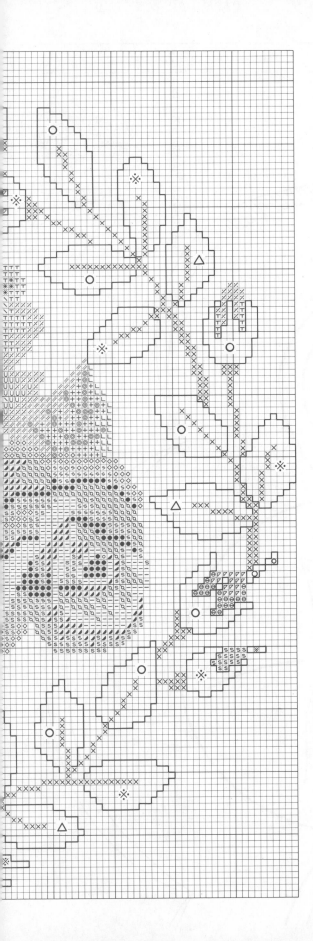

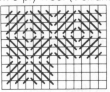
·=7132	⊚=7890
‖=7204	V=7386
⊿=7205	+=7769
⋌=7210	L=7583
⊖=7212	I=7771
■=7375	⊘=7364
⟍=7191	O=7542 ((7485))
⫽=7761	✳=7541 ((7487))
T=7759	△=7540 ((7477))
U=7758	✕=7467
✳=7207 back	
◢=7115 ground = 7928 ((7460))	
−=7745	
◇=7727	(( )) for Brown pillow
◻=7726	
S=7784	(square of design =
◿=7782	thread square of fabric)
●=7781	

95

You'll Need

Fabric... Light weight White linen 40cm square.

Threads...D.M.C 6-strand embroidery floss:

5 skeins of White. Abroder No. 18 White 1 skein.

Finished Size: Refer to chart.

Making Instructions

Arrange design in position referring to chart, work embroidery. Work outline with closed buttonhole stitch using Abroder 1 strand, cut off the surplus.

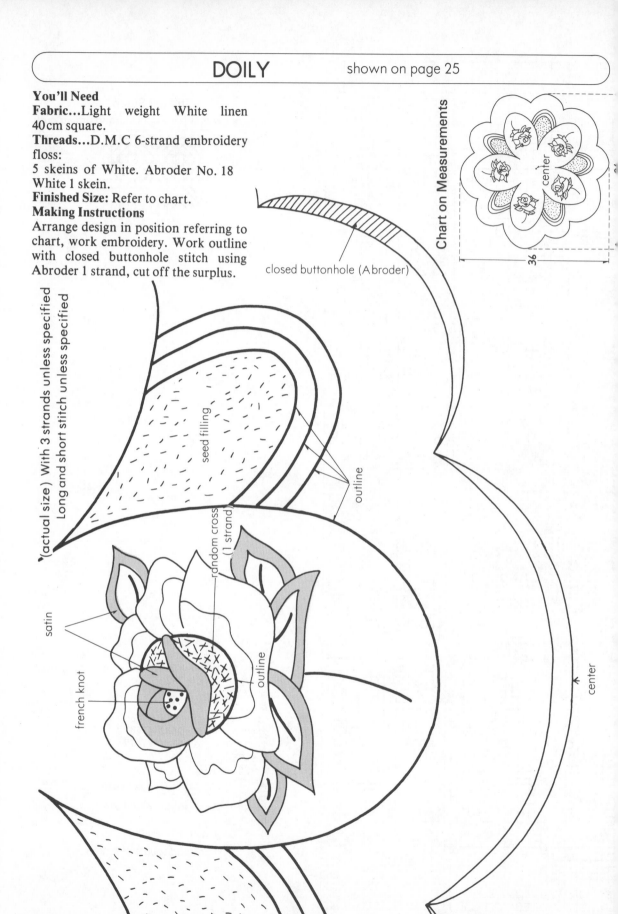

Chart on Measurements

center

36

closed buttonhole (Abroder)

(actual size) With 3 strands unless specified
Long and short stitch unless specified

seed filling

outline

random cross
(1 strand)

outline

satin

french knot

center

You'll Need

Fabric... Light weight White linen 115 cm by 40 cm.

Threads...D.M.C 6-strand embroidery floss: 5 skeins of White. No. 8 embroidery floss 2 balls of White.

Finished Size: 105 cm by 32.5 cm

Making Instructions

Enlarge design, apply on fabric, work with White thread. Work outline with closed buttonhole stitch using No. 8 embroidery floss, cut off the surplus.

Chart on Measurements

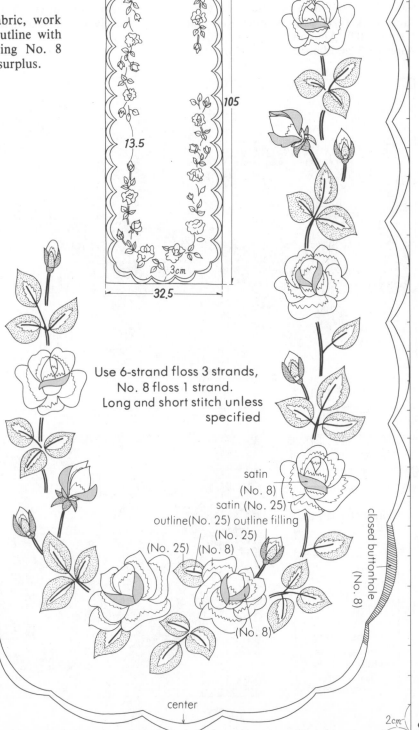

105

13.5

3cm

32.5

Use 6-strand floss 3 strands,
No. 8 floss 1 strand.
Long and short stitch unless
specified

satin
(No. 8)
satin (No. 25)
outline(No. 25) outline filling
(No. 25)
(No. 25) (No. 8)

closed buttonhole
(No. 8)

(No. 8)

center

2cm

LAMPSHADE

shown on page 29

You'll Need

Fabric... Single mesh canvas (6 threads per 1 cm) 10 cm by 1 m.

Threads...D.M.C 6-strand embroidery floss: 20 skeins of Ecru; 2 skeins each of Pistachio Green (367), Almond Green (503), Geranium Pink (893, 894); 1 skein each of Cerise (600, 602, 603, 604, 605), Garnet Red (309, 335), Soft Pink (776, 818), Garnet Red (326), Ivy Green (500), Almond Green (502, 504), Myrtle Grey (926) and Laurel Green (986).

Fittings... Brown velveteen 40 cm by 1 m. 0.8 cm wide ribbon Wine Red 2 m long.

Finished Size: Refer to chart.

Making Instructions

Work half-cross stitch on canvas with 6 strands. Having worked whole pattern, fill background 62 threads in width with Ecru.

Work 4 patterns in series on canvas.

Have it finished in lampshade at specialty store.

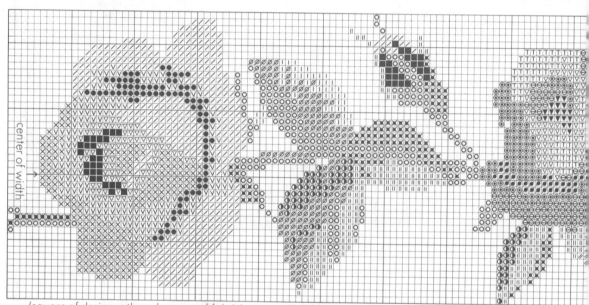

(square of design = thread square of fabric)

▼=600	V=335	◨=986
▨=602	⁄=893	O=367
⊙=603	X=894	◑=502
⊖=604	X=776	∅=503
T=605	▽=818	II=926
■=326	X=500	I=504
●=309	fill background with Ecru	

Finished Diagram

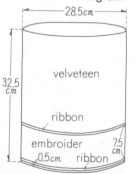

28.5cm

32.5 cm

velveteen

ribbon

embroider 7.5 cm

0.5cm ribbon

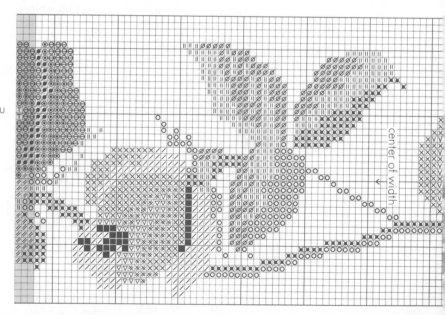

DOILY

shown on page 30 above

You'll Need

Fabric... Light weight White linen 70cm by 40cm.
Threads...D.M.C 6-strand embroidery floss:
2 skeins each of Old Gold (676, 729), Almond Green (502, 503, 504); 1 skein each of Azure Blue (775), Antique Blue (932), Pistachio Green (368), Smoke Grey (644), Soft Pink (819), Faded Pink (221, 223, 224, 225), Ash Grey (317, 318, 414, 415), Cream (746), Old Gold (677) and White.

Finished Size: 68cm by 36cm in oval

Making Instructions

Apply design on fabric referring to chart, embroider with 2 strands. Work outline with closed buttonhole stitch, cut off the surplus.

Chart on Measurements

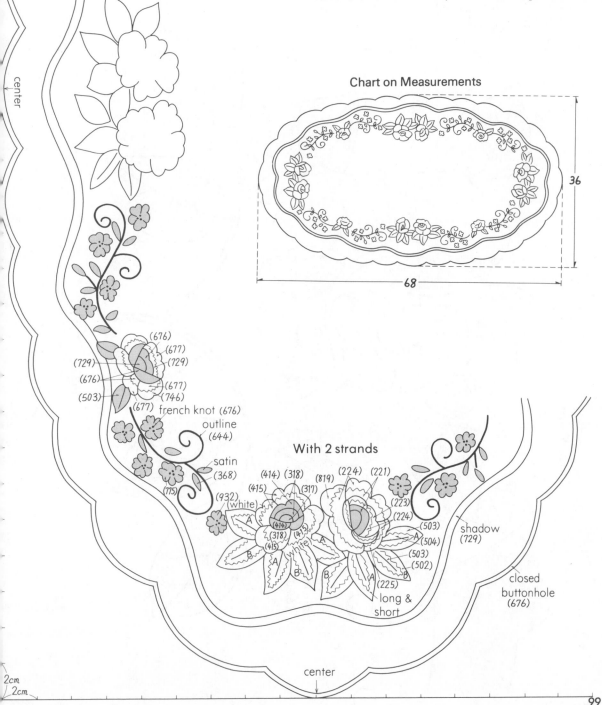

With 2 strands

99

You'll Need

Fabric... Light weight linen: White, Beige 42 cm square each.

Threads...D.M.C 6-strand embroidery floss: 3 skeins each of Dark Brown (3032), Smoke Grey (640) and Beige (3024).

Finished Size: Refer to chart.

(actual size)

satin with 2 strands (640)

beige

beige

outline with 1 strand (3032)

outline with 2 strands (3032)

satin with 2 strands (3032)

punchwork with 1 strand (3024)

satin with 2 strands (640)

Making Instructions

Cut White piece and Beige piece putting 0.5 cm seam allowance.

Finish out edges of each piece turning allowance to wrong side, join with punchwork. Cut out pattern pieces with 0.3 cm allowance, punchwork in position.

Chart on Measurements

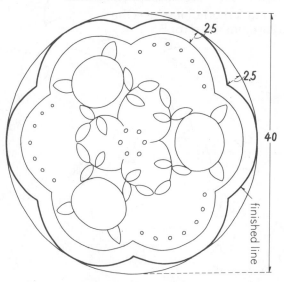

2.5

2.5

40

finished line

PILLOWS shown on page 31

You'll Need (for each)

Fabrics... Wool gabardine Dark Brown 42 cm square. Velveteen Brown 90 cm by 92 cm.

Threads...D.M.C 6-strand embroidery floss:

For A 1 skein each of Golden Yellow (781, 782, 783), Mahogany (402), Aprikot Pink (945, 951), Terra-cotta (355), Red Brown (919, 920, 921, 922), Sage Green (3011, 3012), Yellow Green (730, 732, 733), Umber (738), Drab (612); small amount each of Copper Green (832), Old Gold (676, 677, 729), Coffee Brown (938) and Saffron (725). 2 skeins of Gold thread.

For B 1 skein each of Terra-cotta (355, 356, 758), Dull Mauve (778), Faded Pink (221, 223, 224), Green (3051, 3052), Yellow Green (730, 732), Drab (611), Raspberry Red (3685); small amount each of Chestnut (950), Geranium Red (754), Golden Yellow (783), Dull Mauve (316) and Old Rose (3350). 2 skeins of Gold thread.

Fittings...41 cm long zip. 600 g of cased in kapok. Cotton string 350 cm long. Dark Brown braid 1 m long.

Finished Size: 50 cm in diameter

Making Instructions

Apply enlarged design on gabardine, work embroidery. Cut out back piece and side piece from velveteen, join 4 strips of side together into round, sew referring to chart.

Cutting

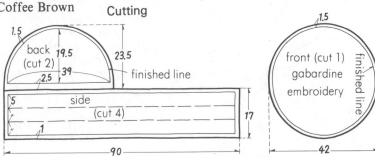

1.5

back (cut 2) 19.5
39
2.5
23.5
finished line

5 side (cut 4) 1
90
17

1.5
front (cut 1) gabardine embroidery
finished line
42

Finished Diagram

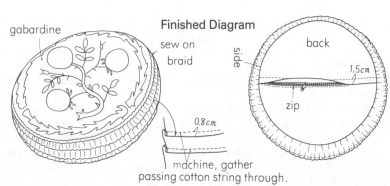

gabardine

sew on braid

0.8 cm

machine, gather passing cotton string through.

side

back

1.5 cm

zip

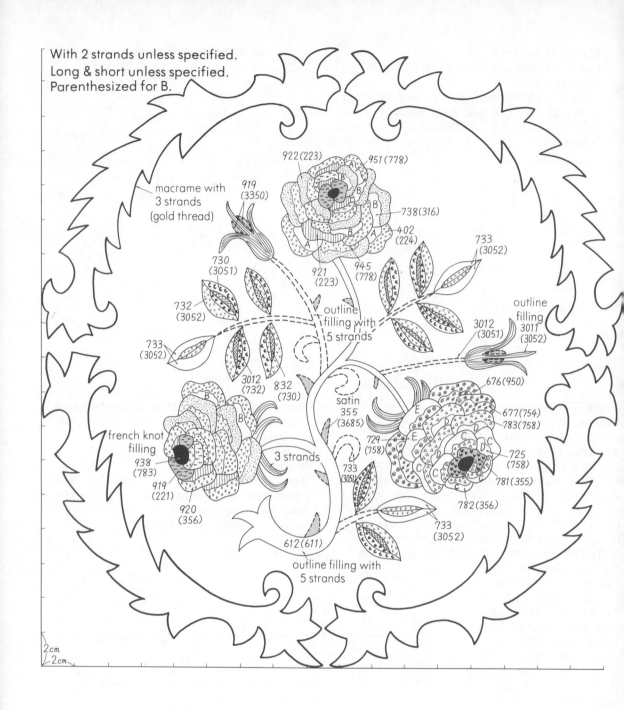

With 2 strands unless specified.
Long & short unless specified.
Parenthesized for B.

macrame with
3 strands
(gold thread)

919
(3350)

922(223)   951(778)

A
B
B
B
B   738(316)

402
(224)
A
A
B

921
(223)   945
(778)

733
(3052)

730
(3051)

732
(3052)

733
(3052)

outline
filling with
5 strands

3012
(3051)

outline
filling
3011
(3052)

3012
(732)   832
(730)

satin
355
(3685)

676(950)

677(754)
783(758)

E
D
E
C   D
C   D
D   C
C   D
C   C
C   D
C   C

725
(758)

781(355)

782(356)

729
(758)

733
(3052)

french knot
filling

938
(783)

919
(221)

920
(356)

B
B

3 strands

733
(3051)

612(611)

outline filling with
5 strands

733
(3052)

2cm
2cm

<hr>

ALBUM   shown on page 32

You'll Need

Fabric...Single mesh canvas (6 threads per 1 cm)
25 cm by 20 cm.

Threads...D.M.C 6-strand embroidery floss:
4 skeins of Umber (739); 1/2 skein each of
Pistachio Green (319, 320, 367, 368, 890),
Laurel Green (989), Scarlet (498, 814, 815,
816), Geranium Red (349, 350, 351, 817),
Turkey Red (321) and Geranium Pink (891,

893, 894).

Fittings...Brown leather 72 cm by 42 cm.
Finished Size: 29 cm wide 34 cm long.
Making Instructions
Work half-cross stitch with 5 strands.
Work background with Beige, extending stitches
for about 10 threads all around.
Have it finished in album at specialty store.

102

(square of design = thread square of fabric)

△ =351 ∕∕ =350 ◑ =349 ▲ =817 ◯ =321 ■ =814 ● =815 ◉ =816 V =498

✚ =891 ∕ =893 ─ =894 ◪ =890 L =319 X =367 X =320 T =368 ⅄ =989 □ =739

BOOKMARKER   shown on page 33 above

You'll Need
Fabric...Sharkskin 9 cm by 8 cm (for each).
Threads...D.M.C 6-strand embroidery floss:
Pink small amount each of Soft Pink (899, 3326), Garnet Red (309, 335, 326) and Cerise (600). **Blue** small amount each of Forget-me-not Blue (826), Sevres Blue (798), Sky Blue (517, 518, 519) and Peacock Blue (807).

Fittings...Small amount of iron-on interfacing.
Finished Size: Refer to chart.
Making Instructions
Work referring to chart, outline with buttonhole stitch. Attach interfacing on wrong side, cut pattern out.

(actual size)   Work outward of long and short stitch with 3 strands, inward with 2 strands.

Long and short stitch unless specified

( )=Pink

[ ]=Blue

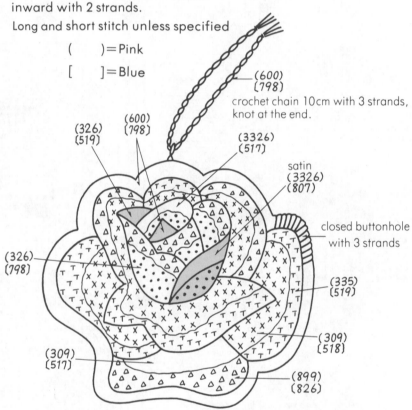

(600)
(798)
crochet chain 10cm with 3 strands, knot at the end.

(326)
(519)

(600)
(798)

(3326)
(517)

satin
(3326)
(807)

(326)
(798)

closed buttonhole with 3 strands

(335)
(519)

(309)
(518)

(309)
(517)

(899)
(826)

JEWELRY BOX   shown on page 33 below

You'll Need
Fabric...Single mesh canvas (6 threads per 1 cm) 30 cm by 20 cm Beige.
Threads...D.M.C 6-strand embroidery floss:
7 skeins of Smoke Grey (822); 1 skein each of Antique Blue (932, 3325), Moss Green (470, 937), Old Gold (676, 677, 680, 729), Myrtle Grey (926, 927), Saffron (727), Ivy Green (500, 501), Almond Green (502, 503, 504), Myrtle Grey (924, 928), Raspberry Red (3685, 3687, 3688, 3689), Old Rose (3350, 3354), Soft Pink

(818, 819) and Magenta Rose (961, 962).
Fittings...Box for jewelry suitable to the size of decoration 21 cm by 13 cm.
Making Instructions
Work half-cross stitch with 6 strands referring to chart. Work background up to required measurements, fix in jewelry box.

(square of design = thread square of fabric)

□ =822   ■ =932   ● =3325   ✖ =3685   / =470   ✚ =937   ⊖ =677   ✖ =729   ✕ =3689   △ =3687   / =3688   ⊕ =501   L =727   ⟨ =676   ✕ =680   ▲ =927   ⟩ =503   ✖ =502   ⊠ =504   ⊓ =924   / =926
A =500   S =928   ● =3350   ● =3350   V =961   ⟨ =818   ≡ =962   △ =819   ○ =3354

center

center

105

BAG

shown on page 34 above

You'll Need

Fabric... Single mesh canvas (6 threads per 1 cm) 60 cm by 25 cm.

Threads...D.M.C 6-strand embroidery floss:

10 skeins of Black (310); 3 skeins of Garnet Red (326); 2 skeins each of Geranium Red (349), Copper Green (830), Soft Pink (899); 1-1/2 skeins each of Sage Green (3012), Moss Green (937), Yellow Green (734), Pistachio Green (320), Garnet Red (335), Geranium Red (350, 351); 1 skein each of Soft Pink (3326), Yellow Green (732), Copper Green (832), Moss Green (471), Geranium Red (352); small amount of Scarlet (816).

Finished Size: Refer to chart.

Making Instructions

Cut out 2 pieces of 30 cm by 25 cm, work half-cross stitch from center with 6 strands. Work background with Black.

Decorate 2 pieces in same manner. Have them fixed in bag at specialty store.

Finished Diagram

16.5 cm

15 cm

20 cm

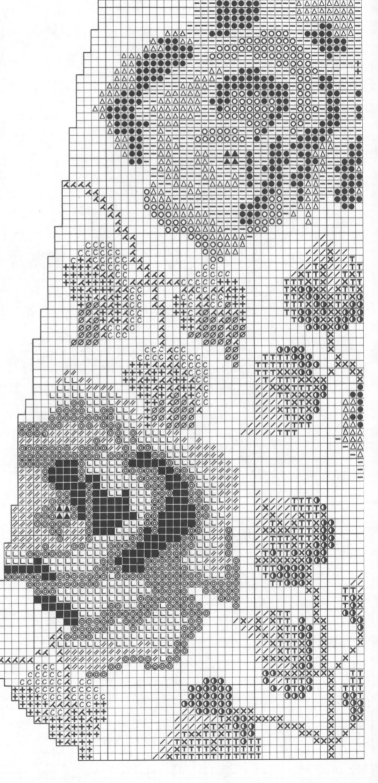

◯ = 3326	⊘ = 351
△ = 899	⊔ = 350
● = 335	◎ = 349
─ = 326	∅ = 471
╱ = 734	╋ = 732
T = 320	C = 832
◖ = 3012	⤢ = 937
✕ = 830	▲ = 816
■ = 352	☐ = 310 (black)

(square of design = thread square of fabric)

106

center

ATOMIZER shown on page 34 below

You'll Need

Fabric...Single mesh canvas (8 threads per 1 cm) 6 cm square.

Threads...D.M.C 6-strand embroidery floss: small amount each of Black (310), Garnet Red (309, 326, 335), Soft Pink (776), Sky Blue (517, 518), Brilliant Green (701, 703) and Tangerine Yellow (743).

Fittings...Pre-made atomizer suitable to the size of decoration 2 cm wide by 4.2 cm long.

Making Instructions

Work half-cross stitch with 3 strands referring to chart, fill background with Black, fix in position.

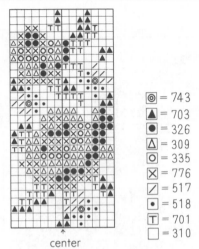

◎	= 743
▲	= 703
●	= 326
△	= 309
◯	= 335
✕	= 776
╱	= 517
•	= 518
T	= 701
☐	= 310

center

(square of design = thread square of fabric)

HAND-MIRROR AND MINI HANGER shown on page 35 below

You'll Need

Fabric...Single canvas (8 threads per 1 cm) 10 cm square for hand-mirror, 5 cm square for mini hanger.

Threads...D.M.C 6-strand embroidery floss: small amount each of Ecru, Faded Pink (221, 223, 224, 225), Dull Mauve (316) and Drab (610, 611, 612).

Fittings...Pre-made hand-mirror suitable to the size of decoration 5.5 cm wide by 6.5 cm long. Pre-made hanger suitable to the size of decoration 3 cm in diameter.

Making Instructions

Work half-cross stitch with 3 strands, fill background with Ecru, fix in position.

Mini hanger

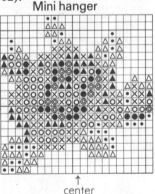

↑
center

◯	= 225
✕	= 224
▲	= 223
●	= 221
◎	= 316
△	= 612
•	= 611
╱	= 610
☐	= Ecru

(square of design = thread square of fabric)

Hand-mirror

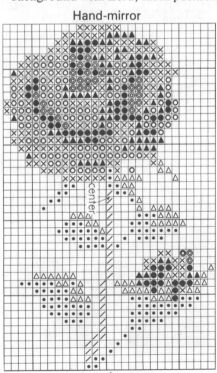

↑
center

108

You'll Need (for each)
Fabric...Linen (12 threads per 1 cm) 5 cm square.
Threads...D.M.C 6-strand embroidery floss:
For Pink
small amount each of Soft Pink (818, 3326), Garnet Red (326, 335), Scarlet (498, 814), Pistachio Green (320, 368, 369, 890) and Smoke Grey (822). **For Brown** small amount each of Umber (433, 434, 435, 436, 437, 738, 739),

Smoke Grey (822), Coffee Brown (898, 938) and Sepia (3371).
Fittings...Pre-made brooch suitable to the size of decoration 3 cm in diameter.
Making Instructions:
Work half-cross stitch with 3 strands.

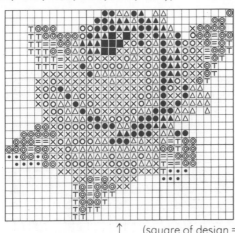

	for pink	for brown
O =	818	739
⊟ =	890	938
⊠ =	3326	437
△ =	335	435
● =	326	433
▲ =	498	898
■ =	814	3371
◎ =	320	434
T =	368	436
• =	369	738
□ =	822	822

↑ center

(square of design = thread square of fabric)

You'll Need
Fabric...Double mesh canvas (6 threads per 1 cm) 5 cm by 3 cm for bracelet, 6 cm by 5 cm for earring.
Threads...D.M.C 6-strand embroidery floss: small amount each of Soft Pink (776, 818, 899, 3326), Garnet Red (309, 335), Scarlet (815), Parrakeet Green (905, 906), Scarab Green (3345, 3346, 3347) and Black (310).

Fittings...Pre-made bracelet suitable to the size of decoration 3 cm by 1.5 cm. Pre-made earring suitable to the size of decoration 2 cm by 1.5 cm in oval.
Making Instructions
Work half-cross stitch with 3 strands, picking up single thread of fabric so that 1 cm counts 12 threads of single.

Bracelet

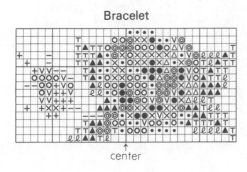

↑ center

Earring

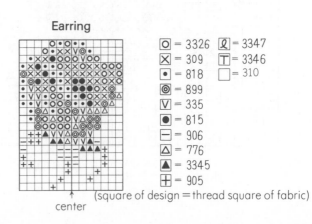

↑ center

O = 3326	ℓ = 3347
⊠ = 309	T = 3346
• = 818	□ = 310
◎ = 899	
V = 335	
● = 815	
⊟ = 906	
△ = 776	
▲ = 3345	
⊞ = 905	

(square of design = thread square of fabric)

FRAME   shown on page 36

You'll Need

Fabric...Oxford (7 threads per 1 cm) Beige 20cm square (for each).

Threads...D.M.C 6-strand embroidery floss:

For Pink 1/2 skein each of Geranium Red (352, 353, 754), Morocco Red (3328), Cardinal Red (347). **For Yellow** 1/2 skein each of Saffron (725, 726, 727), Golden Yellow (782, 783) **For**

Both 1/2 skein each of Moss Green (469, 471, 472, 937), Umber (433), Hazel-nut Blue (420).

Fittings...Frame of 14cm diameter inside.

Finished Size: Same size as frame.

Making Instructions

Apply design on fabric matching centers together, work cross stitch with 3 strands.

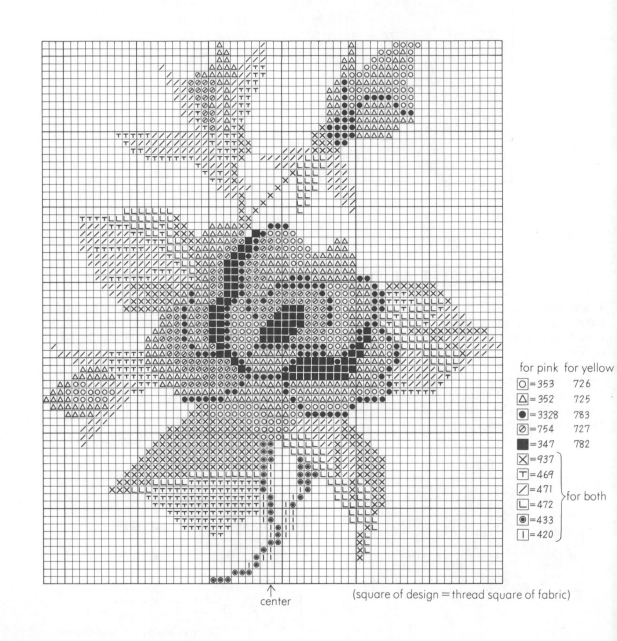

	for pink	for yellow
O =	353	726
△ =	352	725
● =	3328	783
⊘ =	754	727
■ =	347	782
X =	937	
T =	469	
⁄ =	471	for both
L =	472	
◉ =	433	
I =	420	

↑ center

(square of design = thread square of fabric)

110

BEDSPREAD AND PILLOW shown on page 37

You'll Need (2 portions for pillow)
Fabric...For Bedspread Aida cloth (25 threads per 10cm) Beige 90cm by 80cm. Velveteen Dark Moss Green 90cm by 620cm. Broad cloth Dark Moss Green 90cm by 560cm.
For Pillow Eire cloth (35 threads per 10cm) Beige 90cm by 50cm. Velveteen 90cm by 2m.
Threads...D.M.C 6-strand embroidery floss:
For Bedspread 6 skeins of Soft Pink (3326); 5 skeins each of Green (3052), Sage Green (3013), Garnet Red (335); 4 skeins each of Saffron (727), Soft Pink (818); 3 skeins each of Scarlet (498), Poppy (666), Saffron (725), Tangerine Yellow (743), Golden Yellow (783), Moss Green (935), Green (3051), Sage Green (3012); 2 skeins each of Garnet Red (309), Golden Yellow (781), Turkey Red (321), Geranium Pink (892), Scarlet (815), Yellow Green (734); 1 skein each of Scarlet

(902), Ash Grey (415) and White. **For Pillow** half quantity of bedspread use.
Fittings...For Bedspread Dark Green bias tape 250cm long.
For Pillow Bias tape 3m long. 2 of 40cm long zip. Fabric for inner case 90cm by 220cm. 1500g of kapok.
Finished Size: Refer to chart.
Making Instructions
Embroider bedspread with 12 strands. Apply design above the bold line next page on pillow, embroider with 6 strands.
Secure decorated piece on bedspread referring to chart, finish out edge all around sewing together with broad cloth, top stitch steady where indicated.
Sew pillow putting side piece between, set zip in position on back.

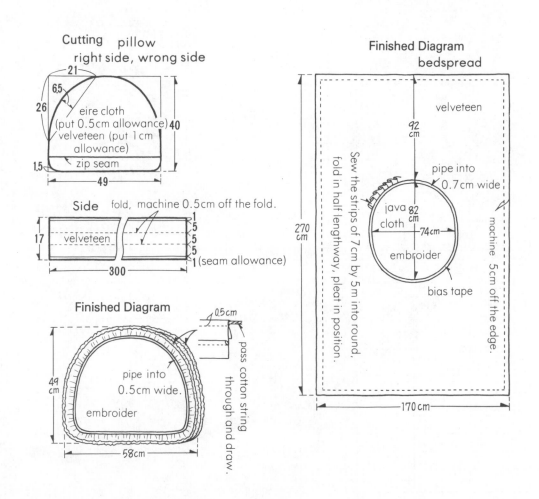

111

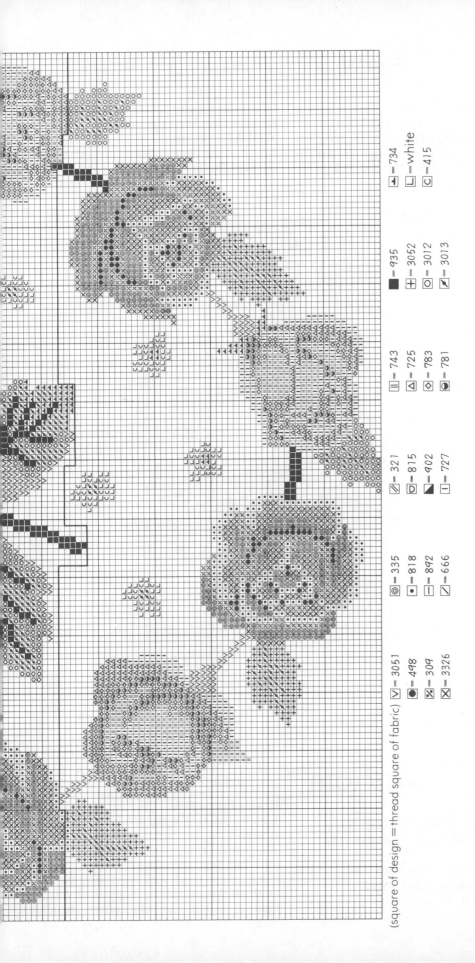

(square of design = thread square of fabric)

∇ = 3051	◎ = 335	⊠ = 321	Ⅲ = 743
● = 498	• = 818	⧄ = 815	△ = 725
⊠ = 309	− = 892	◨ = 902	◇ = 783
⊠ = 3326	⧄ = 666	Ⅰ = 727	◑ = 781

■ = 935	⊣ = 734
+ = 3052	∟ = white
⊙ = 3012	© = 415
◪ = 3013	

You'll Need
Fabric... Beige silk 30 cm by 25 cm.
Threads...D.M.C 6-strand embroidery floss:
small amount each of Old Gold (676, 677, 729),
Copper Green (829, 830), Hazel-nut Brown
(420, 869), Golden Yellow (781, 783) and Yellow

Green (732, 734).
Fittings... Frame of 22 cm by 17 cm inside.
Finished Size: Same size as frame.
Making Instructions
Apply design on center of fabric, work
embroidery, fix in frame.

(actual size)
Long & short unless specified.
With 2 strands unless specified.

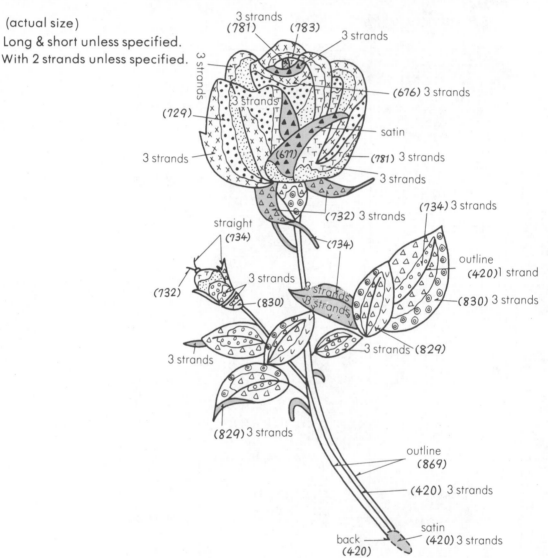

You'll Need
Fabric... White linen (140 cm wide) 55 cm
by 410 cm. Broad cloth Navy Blue 40 cm by
204 cm.
Threads...D.M.C 6-strand embroidery floss:
11 skeins of White; 3 skeins of Indigo (823).
Finished Size: 194 cm by 127 cm

Making Instructions
Seam the pieces of White and Navy Blue together
as shown on the chart, apply design on Navy
Blue, work embroidery. Work open cretan
stitch into 1 cm wide along the seam.
Work outline stitch with Navy Blue on White,
finish all around folding edges twice into 4 cm
wide on wrong side with corners in mitered
shape.

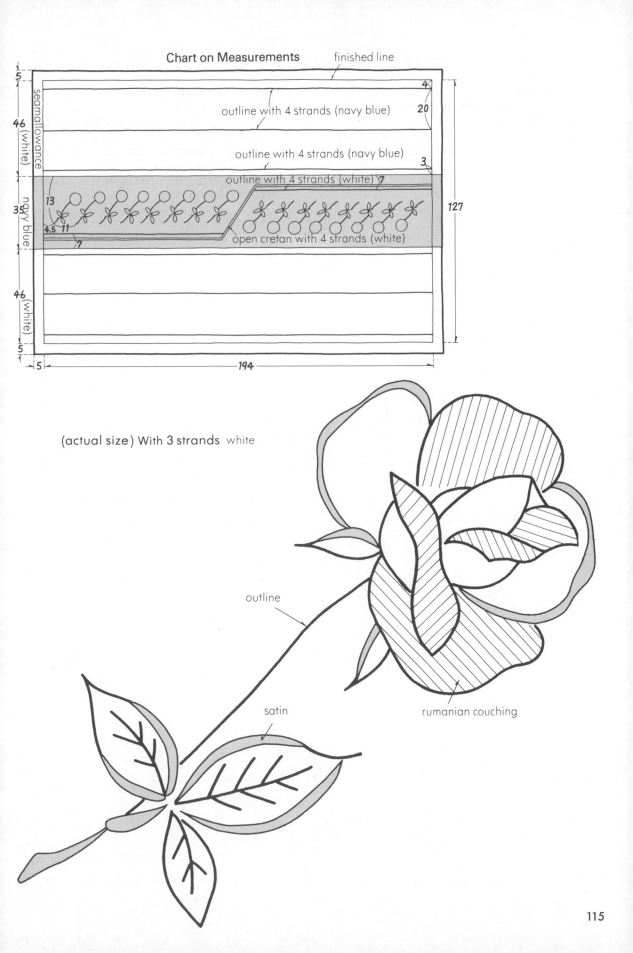

Chart on Measurements

finished line

seamallowance

outline with 4 strands (navy blue)

outline with 4 strands (navy blue)

outline with 4 strands (white)

open cretan with 4 strands (white)

5

46 (white)

35 navy blue

46 (white)

5

4

20

3

7

13

4.5 11

7

127

5

194

(actual size) With 3 strands white

outline

satin

rumanian couching

115

PIANO THROW

shown on page 38 below

You'll Need
Fabric... Light weight linen: White, Beige 92 cm
by 220 cm each.
Threads...D.M.C 6-strand embroidery floss:
2 skeins of White; 1 skein of Smoke Grey (644).

Finished Size: Refer to chart.
Making Instructions
Cut pieces out putting 0.3 cm allowance to the
scalloped edge on the chart, sew edges together
with Beige piece, fold edge piece into shape,
secure with punchwork.
Cut out pattern pieces putting 0.3 cm allowance,
punchwork in position.

Chart on Measurements

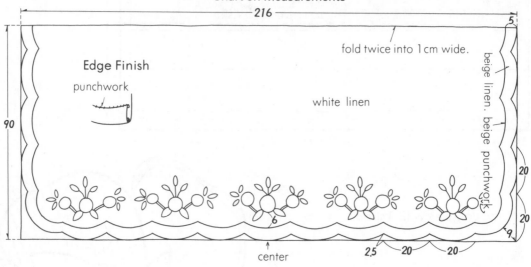

216

fold twice into 1 cm wide.

Edge Finish

punchwork

white linen

beige linen. beige punchwork

90

5

20

20

9

6

center

2.5   20   20

(actual size) With 1 strand unless specified

punchwork (white)

punchwork (644)

shadow (white)

white

satin
(644)
3 strands.

(white)

← center

outline

white

shadow white

beige

see page 75 for punchwork

117

PIANO THROW   shown on page 39

You'll Need
Fabric...Eire cloth (35 threads per 10cm) Beige 216cm by 90cm.

Threads...D.M.C 6-strand embroidery floss:

9 skeins of Coffee Brown (801); 7 skeins of Moss Green (937); 6 skeins each of Saffron (725), Golden Yellow (783), Moss Green (935); 5 skeins of Moss Green (470); 3 skeins each of Beige (3021, 3023), Saffron (726, 727), Golden Yellow (780); 2 skeins each of Almond Green (503), Beige (3022), Tangerine Yellow (745); 1 skein each of Pistachio Green (369), Yellow Green (732) and Ash Grey (762).

Finished Size: 208cm by 82cm

Making Instructions
Reffering to design and the chart on measurements, work cross stitch with 8 strands. Finish out edge mitering at corners.

fold back, finish corners in mitered shape.

Chart on Measurements

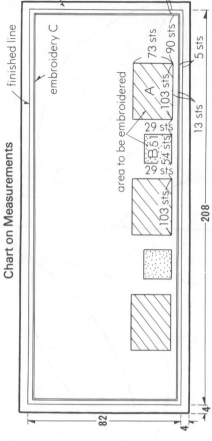

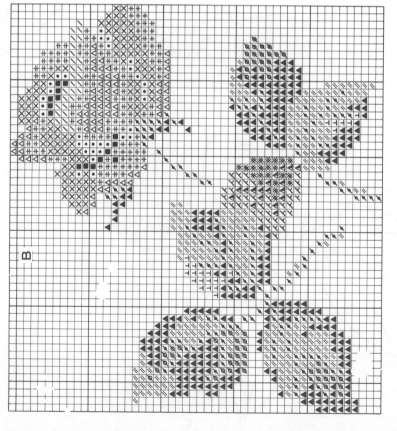

118

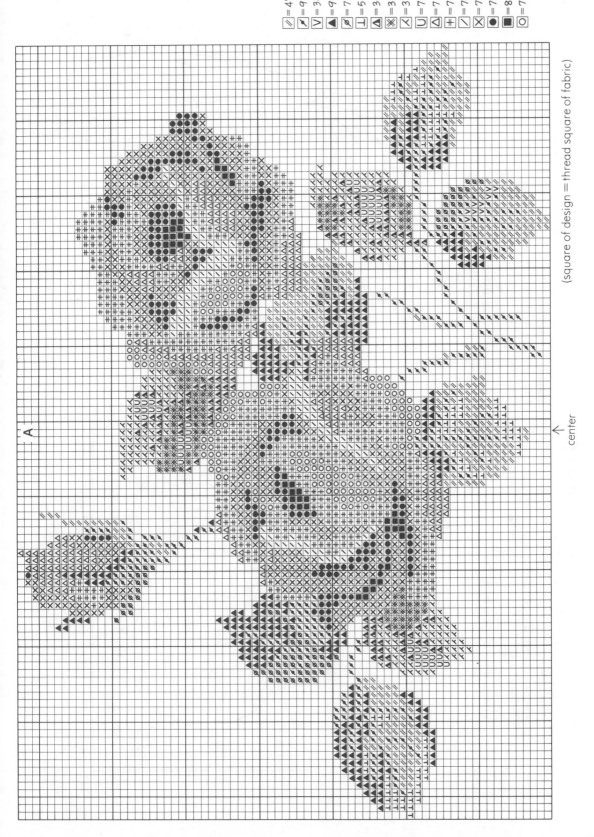

CENTER PIECE

shown on page 40

You'll Need

Fabric... Linen Blue Grey 76cm by 49cm.
Threads...D.M.C 6-strand embroidery floss:
4 skeins of White.
Finished Size: 70cm by 43cm

Making Instructions

The pattern is symmetry except center rose, so apply design half the circle each on fabric. Embroider design, work outline stitch 2.5cm off the edge inward all around.
Turn edges to wrong side, finish corners in mitered shape.

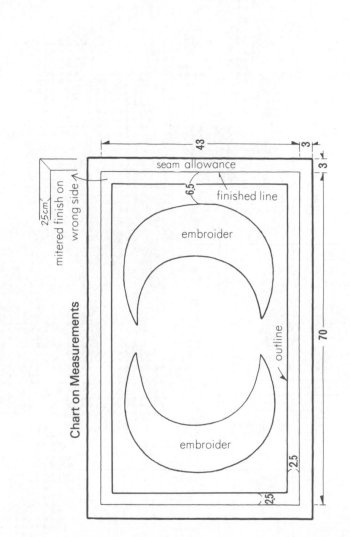

outline with 1 strand

satin

Chart on Measurements

seam allowance

finished line

embroider

outline

embroider

mitered finish on wrong side

25cm

43

6.5

3

3

70

2.5

2.5

long & short

outline

With 2 strands unless specified
(actual size)

center

LUNCHEON SET shown on page 42

You'll Need
Fabric... White linen 148cm by 38cm for runner, 50cm by 40cm for luncheon mat (for each).
Threads...D.M.C 6-strand embroidery floss:

4 skeins each of Tangerine Yellow (742, 743); 2 skeins each of Canary Yellow (971, 972, 973), Scarab Green (3346, 3347), Moss Green (470, 471), Tangerine Yellow (740, 741), Hazelnut Brown (420), Light Yellow (3078); small amount of Tangerine Yellow (745).

Finished Size: Runner 140cm by 30cm
Luncheon Mat 42cm by 32cm
Making Instructions
Embroider applying design referring to chart, finish all around with oneside-hemstitching.

With 3 strands unless specified.

Long & short unless specified.

(actual size)

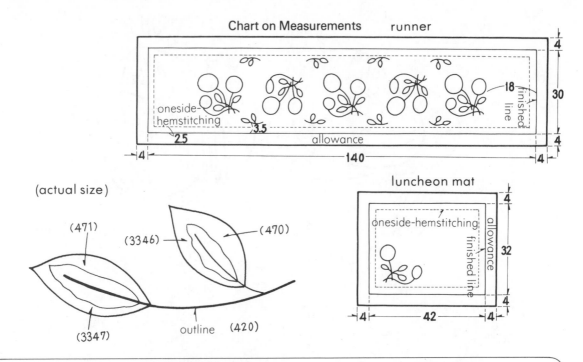

Chart on Measurements   runner

4
18   30
finished line
oneside-hemstitching
2.5   3.5   allowance
4
4   140   4

(actual size)

(471)
(3346)   (470)

(3347)
outline   (420)

luncheon mat

4
oneside-hemstitching
allowance
finished line
32
4
4   42   4

CENTER PIECE   Shown on page 44

You'll Need

Fabric... Linen Navy BLue 41.5 cm by 147 cm.

Threads...D.M.C Retors Abroder No. 4:
5 skeins of White; 3 skeins of Light Blue (2828); 2 skeins of Blue (2799); 1 skein each of Navy Blue (2797, 2827, 2798) D.M.C 6-strand embroidery floss: 3 skeins each of Parrakeet Green (906), Scarab Green (3346); 2 skeins each of Parrakeet Green (904, 905); 1 skein each of Brilliant Green (701, 702, 703, 704), Parrakeet Green (907); small amount each of Sevres Blue (798, 799), Forget-me-not Blue (813), Parma Violet (208, 210), Emerald Green (910) and Peacock Green (992).

Finished Size: 35.5 cm by 141 cm

Making Instructions

Enlarge design, apply 2 patterns as shown, work embroidery. Turn out edge all around twice to wrong side, finish mitering at each corner. Work outline stitch where indicated.

Chart on Measurements

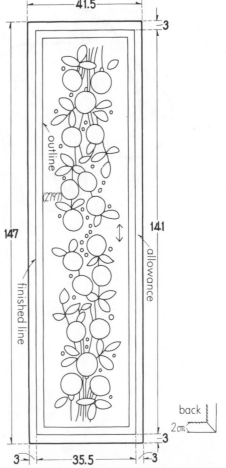

41.5
3
outline
(2799)
147   141
allowance
finished line
back
2cm
3   35.5   3

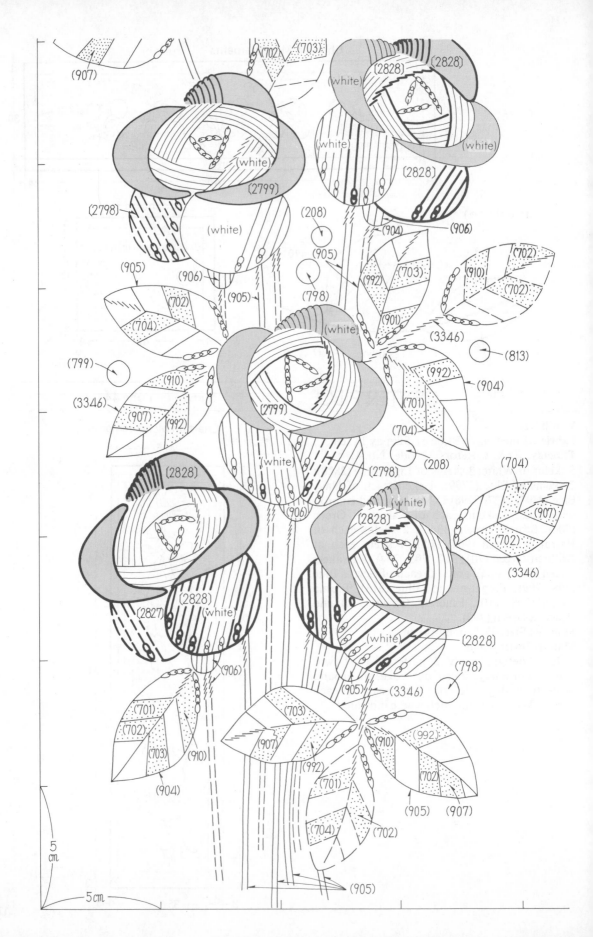

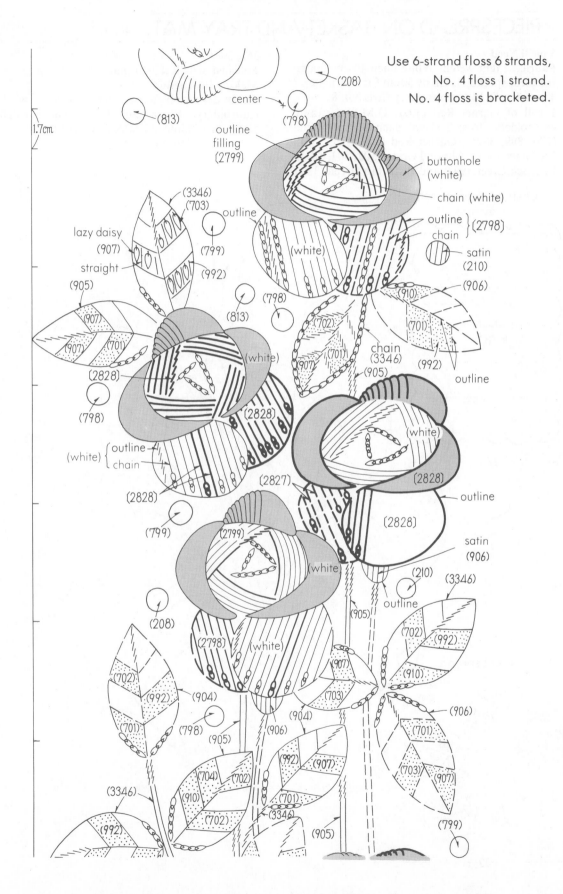

Use 6-strand floss 6 strands,
No. 4 floss 1 strand.
No. 4 floss is bracketed.

(208)

center

(813)

(798)

1.7cm

outline
filling
(2799)

buttonhole
(white)

chain (white)

(3346)
(703)

outline

(799)

(992)

outline
chain } (2798)

satin
(210)

lazy daisy
(907)

straight
(905)

(white)

(906)

(907)

(910)

(906)

(907)

(701)

(701)

(798)

(813)

(702)

(701)

(992)

(2828)

(white)

(907)

chain
(3346)
(905)

outline

(798)

(2828)

(2828)

(white) { outline
         chain

(white)

(2828)

outline

(2827)

(2828)

(2828)

(799)

outline

(2799)

(white)

(2828)

satin
(906)

(208)

(2798)

(white)

(905)

(210)

outline

(3346)

(702)

(992)

(907)

(702)

(992)

(910)

(904)

(903)

(906)

(798)

(905)

(904)

(906)

(907)

(701)

(992)

(907)

(704)

(702)

(703)

(907)

(910)

(701)

(3346)

(702)

(3346)

(992)

(905)

(799)

PIECESPREAD ON BASKET AND TRAY MAT shown on page 43

You'll Need

Fabric... Light weight White linen 40cm square for piece spread, 35cm by 50cm for tray mat.

Threads...D.M.C embroidery floss No. 8: 1 roll of Garnet Red (309). D.M.C 6-strand embroidery floss: 2 skeins each of Soft Pink (776, 899, 3326), Garnet Red (309, 326, 335), Ivy Green (501), Almond Green (502, 503, 504), Peacock Green (992) and Pistachio Green (320,

367, 368).

Finished Size: Refer to chart.

Making Instructions

Apply design on fabric where indicated, work embroidery. Work closed buttonhole stitch along the out line indicated, cut off the surplus.

Chart on Measurements

tray mat

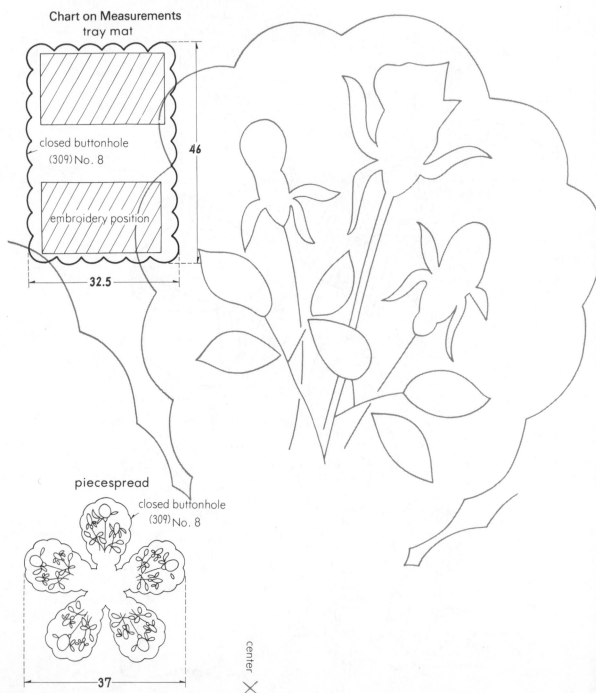

closed buttonhole
(309) No. 8

46

embroidery position

32.5

piecespread

closed buttonhole
(309) No. 8

37

center

126

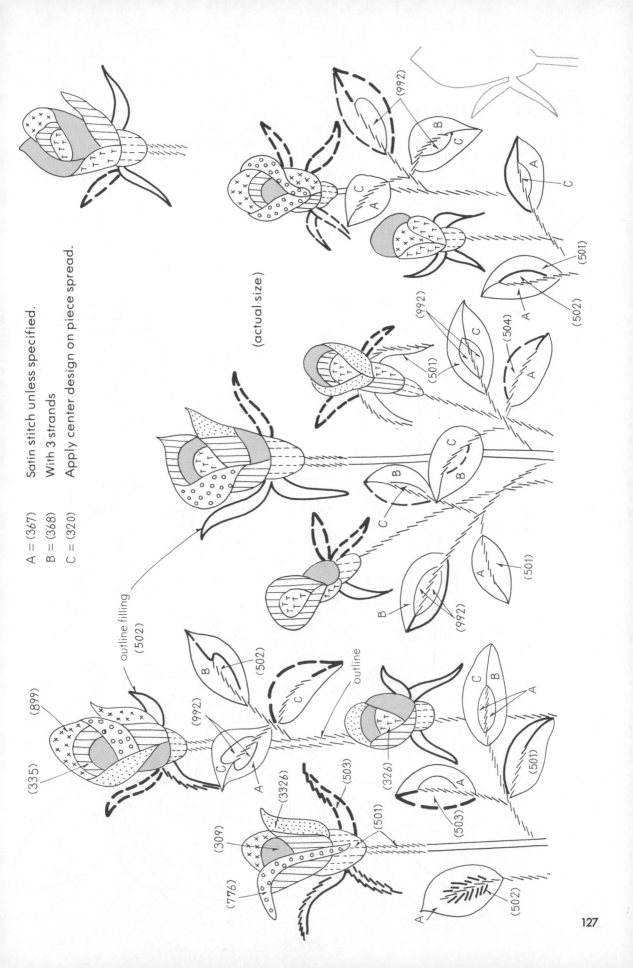

A = (367)
B = (368)
C = (320)

Satin stitch unless specified.
With 3 strands
Apply center design on piece spread.

(actual size)

127

DOILY

shown on page 45 above

You'll Need
Fabric... Red linen 55cm by 35cm.
Threads...D.M.C 6-strand embroidery floss: 8 skeins of White.

Chart on Measurements

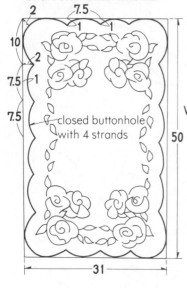

Finished Size: 50cm by 31cm
Making Instructions
Apply design on fabric referring to chart, work embroidery. Work out line of the piece with closed buttonhole stitch, cut off the surplus.

(actual size)
With 3 strands unless specified.

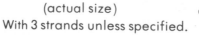

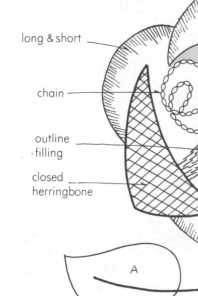

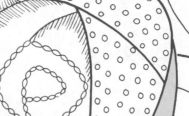

128

SLIPPERS　　shown on page 51

You'll Need (for each pair)
Fabric...Congress (70 threads per 10cm) Grey 78cm by 30cm.
Threads...D.M.C 6-strand embroidery floss
For Pink
1/2 skein each of Old Rose (3350), Peony Rose (956, 957), Soft Pink (818), Scarlet (814) and Cerise (605).
For Blue 1/2 skein each of Royal Blue (797, 995), Sevres Blue (798, 799) and Cornflower Blue (791, 794).

For Both 1/2 skein each of Pistachio Green (319) and Brilliant Green (702, 704).
Finished Size: In standard size.
Making Instructions
Cut pieces out referring to chart, embroider where indicated with 6 strands in required colors, counting 2-thread square as 1 square of fabric. Embroider so that the design on slippers to be finished in symmetry.
Have them finished at specialty store.

Chart on Measurements

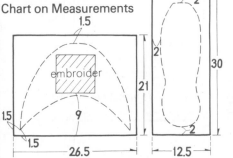

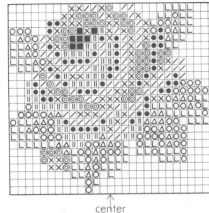

	for pink	for blue
◎	3350	797
✕	956	798
○	818	794
/	957	995
■	814	791
‖	605	799
L		704
○		702
△		319

(square of design = thread square of fabric)

center

work design symmetrically.

PILLOWCASE AND PIECESPREAD　　shown on page 48

You'll Need
Fabric...White linen 90cm by 124cm for pillowcase, 90cm by 140cm for piecespread.
Threads...D.M.C 6-strand embroidery floss:
2 skeins of Drab (613); 1-1/2 skeins each of Forget-me-not Blue (813, 826, 827), Moss Green (470, 471), Scarab Green (3347), Canary Yellow (970, 971); 1 skein each of Pistachio Green (320, 368), Moss Green (472), Fire Red (900, 946), Canary Yellow (972, 973); small amount of Hazel-nut Brown (420).
Fittings...Yellow bias tape 250cm long, 2 pairs of snaps for pillowcase. Yellow bias tape 130cm long for piecespread.
Finished Size: Pillowcase Refer to chart.
Piecespread 128cm by 60cm
Making Instructions
Pillowcase Cut fabric referring to chart, apply design on front, so that patterns arranged in symmetry except center rose, embroider with indicated colors.
Sew into pillowcase putting bias tape and frill between front piece and back piece. Sew snaps on back side.
Piecespread Cut fabric referring to chart, embroider where indicated. Sew on bias tape and frill referring to chart.

Cutting (pillowcase)

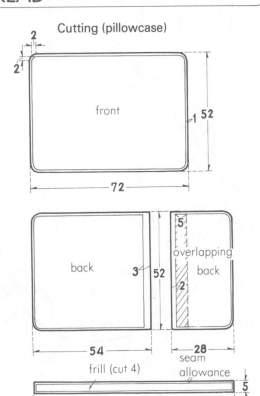

Pillowcase

long &
short
(900)

(972)
(971)
(946)
(970)
(946)
(900)
(972)
(971)
(900)
(970)
(972)
(971)
(970)
(973)
(900)
(970)

(3347)

outline
(420)

closed
herringbone
(613)

center

french (320)
knot
(472)

(826)

(320)

(320)
(813)
(368)

satin
(827)

satin
(368)

(3347)

satin
(471)

(3347)

long &
short
(971)
(471)

(970)

(320)

outline
(613)

With 3 strands unless specified
Inward of long and short with 2 strands

(320)

satin
(470)

(826)
(320)

(320)

(813)

(320)

(320)

Back

snap

17 cm   5cm   5cm   17 cm

Finished
Diagram

50 cm

0.3cm wide bias tape   3cm width

Front

4.5cm

70cm

finish cut edge folding twice.

2 cm
2 cm

130

Chart on Measurements

Piecespread

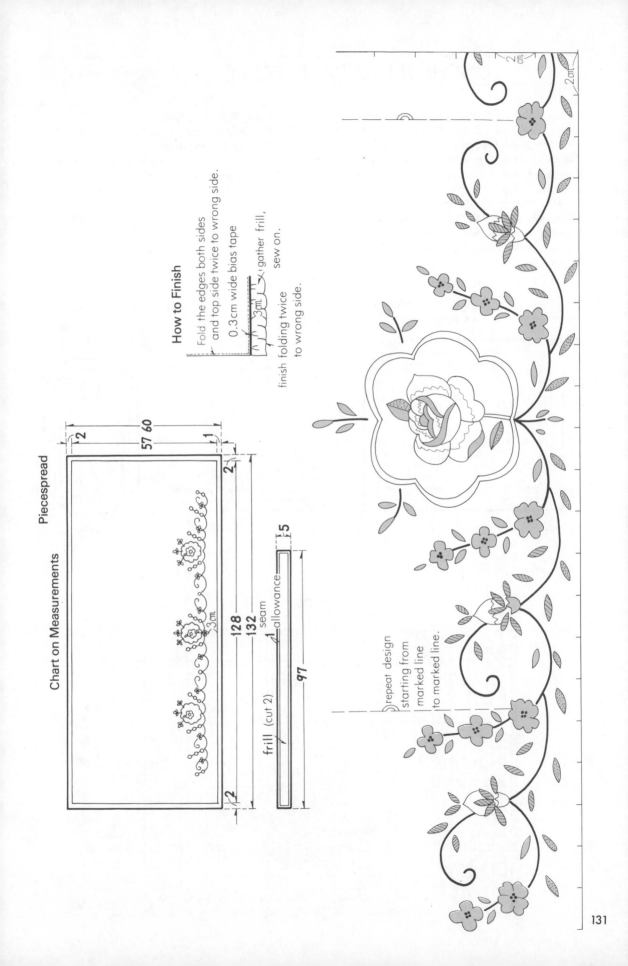

57 60
2
1
2
128
132
3㎝
2
97

frill (cut 2)
seam allowance
F5

How to Finish

Fold the edges both sides
and top side twice to wrong side.

0.3cm wide bias tape

3㎝ gather frill,
sew on.

finish folding twice
to wrong side.

repeat design
starting from
marked line
to marked line.

2㎝
2㎝

LUNCHEON MAT AND DOILY

shown on page 45 below

You'll Need

Fabric... Indian cloth (48 threads per 10 cm) 50 cm by 40 cm for luncheon mat (for each), 23 cm by 37 cm for doily.

Threads...D.M.C 6-strand embroidery floss:

Luncheon Mat 2 skeins each of Pistachio Green (320, 367, 368); 1 skein each of Scarab Green (3346), Umber (433), Tangerine Yellow (740, 741, 742, 743, 744), Light Yellow (3078) and Golden Yellow (783). **Doily** 1 skein each of Umber (433), Pistachio Green (320, 367, 368),

Tangerine Yellow (740, 741, 742, 743, 744) and Light Yellow (3078).

Finished Size: Refer to chart.

Making Instructions

Work cross stitch on luncheon mat and doily referring to chart, finish as shown.

Chart on Measurements

Luncheon Mat

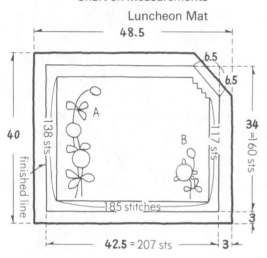

Chart on Measurements

Doily

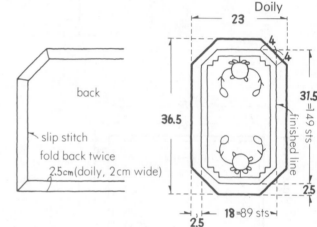

Doily

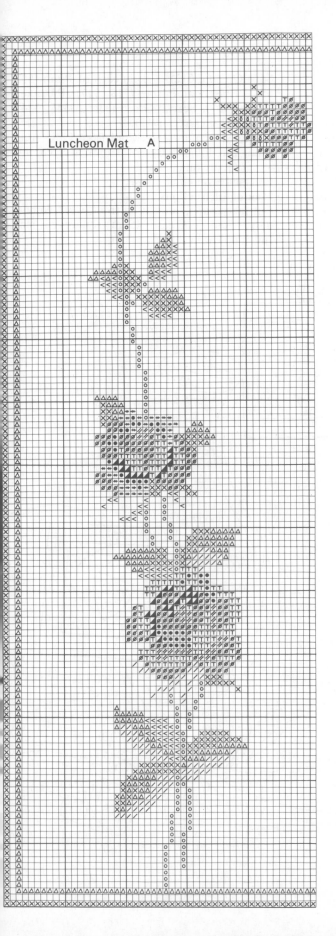

Luncheon Mat A

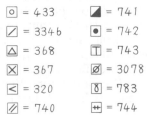

⊡ = 433	◩ = 741
⊘ = 3346	● = 742
△ = 368	⊤ = 743
⊠ = 367	⌀ = 3078
◁ = 320	ঠ = 783
⊘ = 740	⊞ = 744

B (square of design = thread square of fabric)

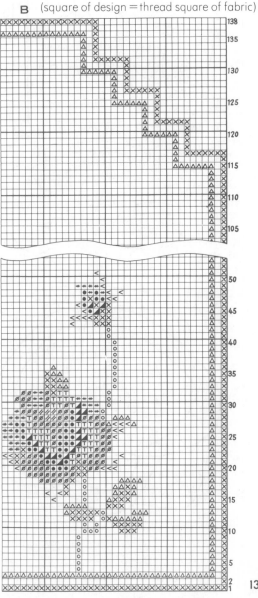

133

PILLOWS

shown on page 46

You'll Need (for each)

Fabric... White linen 45 cm by 95 cm.

Threads... D.M.C 6-strand embroidery floss:

For Pink 1 skein each of Cerise (601, 602, 603, 604), Canary Yellow (971, 972, 973), Peony Rose (956), Scarlet (304) and Fire Red (947).

For Blue 1 skein each of Forget-me-not Blue (826), Sevres Blue (798, 799), Sky Blue (517, 518), Cornflower Blue (791, 792), Royal Blue (996), Plum (553) and Parma Violet (210). **For Both** 2 skeins each of Brilliant Green (702),

Sage Green (3012); 1 skein each of Plum (553, 554), Episcopal Purple (718, 917), Parrakeet Green (907), Scarab Green (3345, 3346, 3347) and Emerald Green (912).

Fittings... 42 cm long zip. Cord Deep Pink (Aqua Blue) 2 m long. 500 g of kapok stuffed into 45 cm square inner case.

Finished Size: 42 cm square

Making Instructions

Cut fabric, apply design on front, work embroidery. Sew innercase 45 cm square in size, finish pillow in shape.

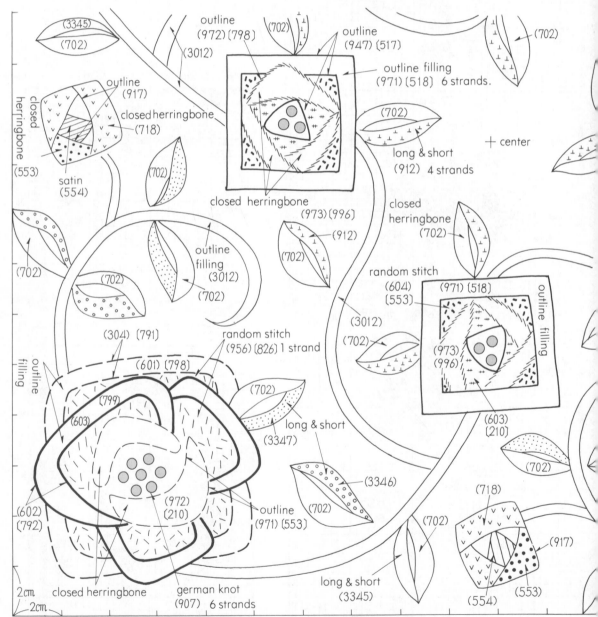

bracketed for Blue pillow

random stitch with 1 strand, leaves and stems with 4 strands, the rest with 6 strands

Cutting

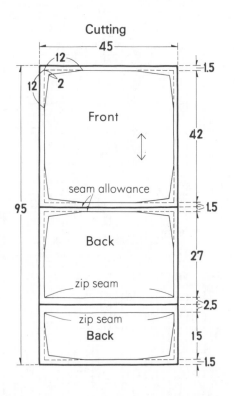

Finished Diagram

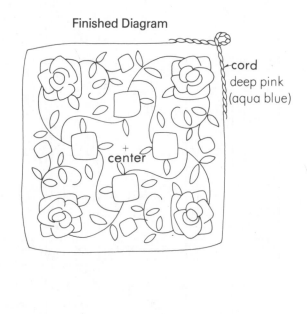

cord
deep pink
(aqua blue)

center

PILLOWS   shown on page 47

You'll Need (for each)

Fabric... Eire cloth (35 threads per 10cm) Beige 90cm by 45cm.

Threads...D.M.C 6-strand embroidery floss:
For Blue 9 skeins of Indigo (336); 4-1/2 skeins of Beaver Grey (647); 1 skein each of Indigo (322), Forget-me-not Blue (813, 827), Sevres Blue (800), Conrnflower Blue (793, 794), Sky Blue (519, 747), Royal Blue (996); 1/2 skein each of Sevres Blue (798, 799), Indigo (312, 334), Forget-me-not Blue (826, 828), Azure Blue (775, 3325), Sky Blue (517, 518), Royal Blue (797) and Peacock Blue (806, 807). **For Pink** 9 skeins of Raspberry Red (3685); 4-1/2 skeins of Ash Grey (318); 1 skein each of Morocco Red (760, 761, 3328), Old Rose (3354), Magenta Rose (962), Raspberry Red (3689), Episcopal Purple (718), Soft Pink (776, 818); 1/2 skein each of Raspberry Red (3687, 3688), Garnet Red (309, 326, 335), Old Rose (3350), Soft Pink (819, 3326) and Cerise (600, 601, 603). **For Both** 1 skein each of Myrtle Grey (926, 927), Ivy Green (501), Peacock Green (991, 992); 1/2 skein each of Almond Green (502, 503), Brilliant Green (701, 703, 704), Myrtle Grey (928); small amount of Myrtle Grey (924).

Fittings...38cm long zip. 500g of cased-in kapok.

Finished Size: 43cm square

Making Instructions

Work cross stitch where indicated with 6 strands. Sew zip on back, finish putting cased-in kapok into.

Cutting

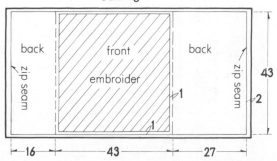

144 stitches

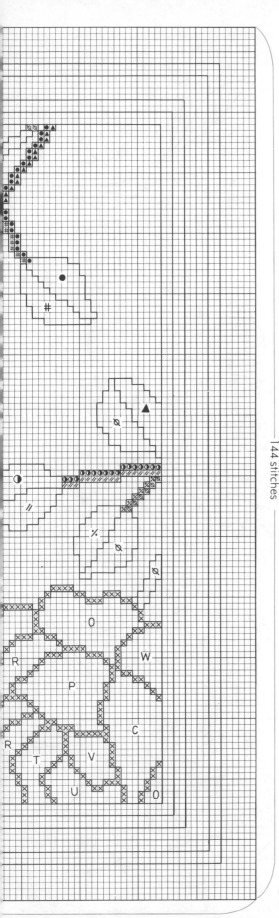

— 144 stitches —

(for both)	(for blue)	(for pink)
⊟ = 992	⊠ = 336	3685
⊞ = 991	Ⓐ = 519	760
◎ = 924	Ⓑ = 747	761
⊞ = 928	Ⓒ = 647	318
△ = 927	Ⓓ = 996	718
● = 926	Ⓔ = 518	3328
◑ = 704	Ⓕ = 517	600
□ = 703	Ⓖ = 806	601
▲ = 701	Ⓗ = 807	603
⊠ = 503	Ⓘ = 800	3689
⊘ = 502	Ⓙ = 798	3687
⊠ = 501	Ⓚ = 799	3688
	Ⓛ = 794	3354
	Ⓜ = 797	3350
	Ⓝ = 793	962
	Ⓞ = 813	776
	Ⓟ = 827	818
	Ⓠ = 828	819
	Ⓡ = 334	309
	Ⓢ = 3325	3326
	Ⓣ = 322	335
	Ⓤ = 826	3350
	Ⓥ = 312	326
	Ⓦ = 775	819

(square of design = thread square of fabric)

outline filling (839)

(842)

(841)

4 strands

(840)

(838)
(839)
(840)
With 6 strands unless specified.
Outline unless specified.

3 cm

3 cm

You'll Need (for each)
Fabrics... Wool 54 cm by 62 cm of Brown, 54 cm by 30 cm of Beige.
Threads...D.M.C 6-strand embroidery floss:
3 skeins of Beige Brown (839); 2 skeins each of Beige Brown (838, 840); 1 skein each of Beige Brown (841, 842).

Fittings...40 cm long zip. 750 g of cased-in kapok.
Finished Size: 50 cm by 40 cm
Making Instructions
Enlarge design, apply on Beige piece, embroider with outline stitch.
Sew into pillow referring to chart.

Chart on Measurements

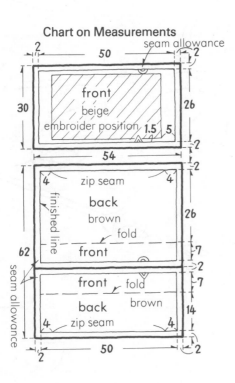

Finished Diagram

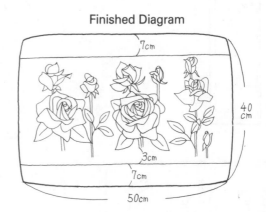

BEDSPREAD   shown on page 49

You'll Need
Fabric... Heavy weight Pink satin (130 cm wide) 130 cm by 590 cm.
Threads...D.M.C Retors Abroder No. 4:
11 skeins of Light Rose (2574), 9 skeins of Dark Rose (2570), 5 skeins of Rose (2572), 2 skeins of White and 1 skein of Pale Pink (2818).
Fittings... Broad cloth for lining 90 cm by 310 cm.
1.5 cm wide braid Deep Rose 670 cm long.
Finished Size: Refer to chart.

Making Instructions
Cut fabric referring to chart, apply enlarged design on the fabric where indicated, embroider with 1 strand.
Sew decorated piece and gathered frill right sides together, inserting braid between.
Sew lining on wrong side of the decorated piece.

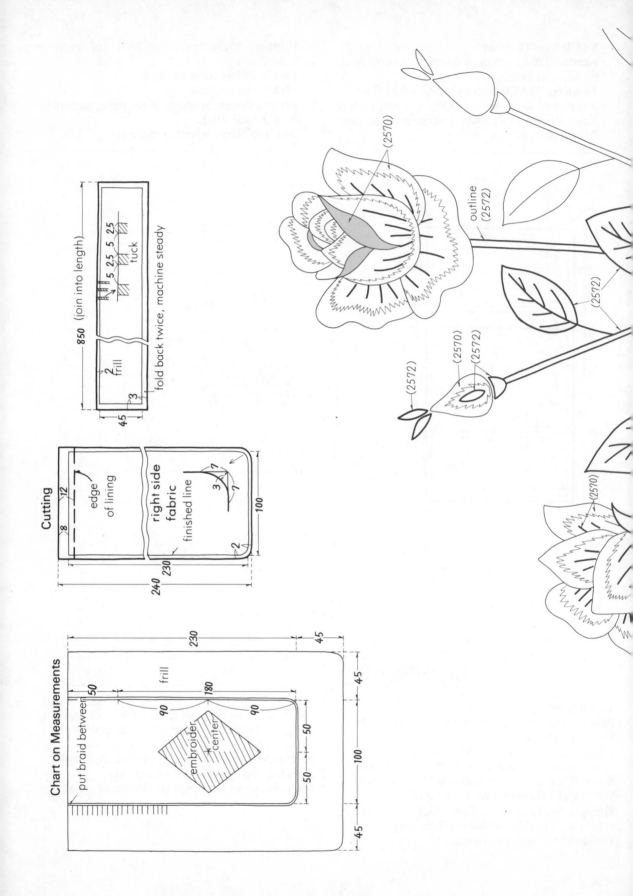

Cutting

850 (join into length)

5 2.5 5 2.5

tuck

frill

fold back twice, machine steady

edge of lining

right side fabric

finished line

Chart on Measurements

put braid between

frill

embroider

center

(2574)

outline (2818)

long & short (white)

satin (white)

center

(2572)

(2574)

(2574)

(2574)

(2574)

(2572)

(2570)

(2572)

(2572)

(2574)

(2570)

4 cm.

4 cm.

141

RUG

You'll Need

Fabric... Bengaline cloth 98 cm by 68 cm.

Threads...D.M.C Tapisserie wool:
8 skeins of Episcopal Purple (7157); 5 skeins of Emerald Green (7911); 4 skeins each of Indigo (7318), Brilliant Green (7943), Emerald Green (7912, 7954); 3 skeins each of Cerise (7153), Indigo (7314); 2 skeins each of Raspberry Red (7151), Cerise (7602, 7605), White; 1 skein each of Cornflower Blue (7247), Blue Purple (7243), Cerise (7136), Episcopal Purple (7155), Antique Blue (7302), Azure Blue (7800), Reddish Brown (7255), Navy Blue (7316), Dark Blue (7306) and Peacock Blue (7995).

Fittings... Rug (or heavy weight wool fabric) for interfacing 92 cm by 62 cm. Urethan for lining 93 cm by 63 cm.

Finished Size: 92 cm by 62 cm